Unpacking Privilege in the Elementary Classroom

Brimming with reflection and resources, this book is ideal for white elementary teachers who wish to host conversations about race with their predominantly white classes.

This book is a clear-cut guide for integrating antiracism into teaching and education, along with policy reform needed for systemic change. Providing hands-on experience and practical insights from literature, it breaks down subject-specific strategies to approach racial conversations. This book acknowledges the variety of challenges that teachers face and encourages them to continue self-work as a step toward supporting students.

While specifically targeting all-white and predominantly white classrooms, this resource is suitable for additional professional development and educator preparation programs when considering a variety of racial dynamics.

Jacquelynne Anne Boivin is Assistant Professor of Elementary and Early Childhood Education at Bridgewater State University, USA.

Kevin McGowan is Associate Professor of Elementary and Early Childhood Education at Bridgewater State University, USA.

Other Eye on Education Books Available from Routledge
(www.routledge.com/eyeoneducation)

Creative Sound Play for Young Learners: A Teacher's Guide to Enhancing Transition Times, Classroom Communities, SEL, and Executive Function Skills
Danny Steele and Todd Whitaker

Everyday STEAM for the Early Childhood Classroom: Integrating the Arts into STEM Teaching
Margaret Loring Merrill

Trauma-Informed Practices for Early Childhood Educators, 2nd Edition: Relationship-Based Approaches that Reduce Stress, Build Resilience and Support Healing in Young Children
Julie Nicholson, Linda Perez, Julie Kurtz, Shawn Bryant, Drew Giles

Unpacking Privilege in the Elementary Classroom
A Guide to Race and Inequity for White Teachers

Jacquelynne Anne Boivin with Kevin McGowan

NEW YORK AND LONDON

Cover image: Getty Images

First published 2025
by Routledge
605 Third Avenue, New York, NY 10158

and by Routledge
4 Park Square, Milton Park, Abingdon, Oxon, OX14 4RN

Routledge is an imprint of the Taylor & Francis Group, an informa business

© 2025 Jacquelynne Anne Boivin with Kevin McGowan

The right of Jacquelynne Anne Boivin with Kevin McGowan to be identified as authors of this work has been asserted in accordance with sections 77 and 78 of the Copyright, Designs and Patents Act 1988.

All rights reserved. No part of this book may be reprinted or reproduced or utilised in any form or by any electronic, mechanical, or other means, now known or hereafter invented, including photocopying and recording, or in any information storage or retrieval system, without permission in writing from the publishers.

Trademark notice: Product or corporate names may be trademarks or registered trademarks, and are used only for identification and explanation without intent to infringe.

ISBN: 9781032495019 (hbk)
ISBN: 9781032491219 (pbk)
ISBN: 9781003394112 (ebk)

DOI: 10.4324/9781003394112

Typeset in Palatino
by codeMantra

This book is dedicated to my dearest husband, Craig. You always support me in pursuing every dream I conjure. This book wouldn't have been possible without your support and love.

Contents

Foreword..viii

1 My Story and Inspiration.............................1

2 Racial Segregation in America's Schools Today.........19

3 Helping Ourselves Before Helping Our Students.......43

4 The Importance of Support 64

5 Starting Small and Keeping It Real 82

6 ELA Approaches...................................102

7 Math and Science Approaches......................126

8 Social Studies/Civics Approaches....................146

9 Social-Emotional Learning Approaches 168

10 Continuing the Journey and Setting Goals............194

Index..209

Foreword

As elementary and early childhood educators, we lay the foundational groundwork for children's later success in life. We teach children how to read, do math, engage in experiments, explore creativity through the arts, and provide experiences for social-emotional development which later enhances emotional intelligence as children emerge into adulthood. As part of social-emotional development, we teach children how to be empathetic in general. In addition to showing empathy in a general sense for people who are the same as us, especially the same race, white teachers who teach in predominantly white school districts must also be intentional in terms of teaching white children to have empathy for other races. As teachers go about doing this important work, it is happening in overarching systems built upon racism with public educational systems being no exception to this rule.

As we celebrate the triumphs of the 1954 *Brown v. Board of Education* decision, we also must acknowledge the unintended negative consequences which in some ways doubled down on public school segregation. In 2024, 70 years after the Brown decision, schools in our country are still segregated by race because our neighborhoods are still segregated by race. Unfortunately, as we are almost a quarter of the way into the 21st century, children's zip codes still determine the quality of their public school education. For the foreseeable future, white teachers will work in predominantly white schools teaching white children. Since this is the case, this book provides practical insights and strategies for teachers to use across the content areas with an explicit focus on race.

White elementary teachers teaching in predominantly white schools can have very successful careers without addressing racism. To borrow Dr. Boivin's phrase from chapter one, white teachers can remain in the "La La Land of Whiteness." What makes a white early childhood and elementary educator decide to do antiracist work, especially as white teachers teaching white children in white neighborhoods? Dr. Boivin answers this question as she candidly takes us on her personal and professional antiracist journey and how this journey informed her antiracism teaching as an elementary school teacher as well as a teacher educator preparing future elementary teachers.

By Dr. Kevin McGowan

1

My Story and Inspiration

Growing Up in the La La Land of Whiteness

"How would you best describe the elementary school you attended growing up?"

This question brings a wide smile to my face. I think back fondly to the following:

Great playground with lots of structures and space to run.

New computers that had fun games and typing programs.

Teachers who truly cared about their students and went the extra mile.

Yearly fieldtrips to museums, performances, or historical reenactment centers.

Pretty nice-sounding school, right? Well, what I likely should have mentioned was that I was a white student at a predominantly white public school. By stating that racial dynamic, it is almost a given that my initial descriptors would be true. A school with great facilities and faculty are synonymous with a school that is predominantly white in the US. In fact, white school districts in the US receive $23 billion more than nonwhite school districts, while serving the same number of students. Furthermore, "White school districts average revenue receipts of almost $14,000 per student, but nonwhite districts receive only $11,682. That's a divide of over $2,200, on average, per student" (EdBuild, 2019, p. 4). Black students are more likely to attend high-poverty schools, and this is associated with adverse impacts on black students' academic performance (E. García, 2020). Money means resources, and in the US, the money tends to follow white people.

White schools usually mean more than money, they can also mean a more conducive learning environment. Students at low-income schools and with student bodies consisting of minoritized races face stark educational drawbacks compared to students at predominantly white schools. With teachers who hold less experience, contenting with lower academic achievement rates, students at these schools have less of a chance of graduating high school and going to college. Consequently, they are less likely to get good-paying jobs and make less over the span of their careers (Green, 2018).

Racial segregation of school is not a concept of the past. As depicted in Figure 1.0, in the 2018–2019 school year, 79% of white elementary and secondary public school students attended schools where more than half of their peers were also white (Pew Research Center, 2021; Schaeffer, 2021). The same year, 56% of Hispanic students and 47% of black students attended schools where more than half of their peers were of the same race.

In addition, the whiteness of the teaching profession prevails. As of the 2017–2018 academic year, 79% of public school teachers identified as white (non-Hispanic) (National Center for Education Statistics [NECS], 2020). A mere 9% identified as Hispanic and 7% identified as black (non-Hispanic).

As a white student surrounded by white teachers, administrators, and peers, white was the norm. White was the comfortable, stable, status quo that was rarely challenged. It was not until I entered college, when I was surrounded by people from all over the world, that I realized how limited my viewpoint had been. I was awoken to biases that I previously, unconsciously held. I made mistakes around people of color and was called out for them and learned that it was the feedback I needed if I truly wanted to grow. I had to set my ego aside and take criticism

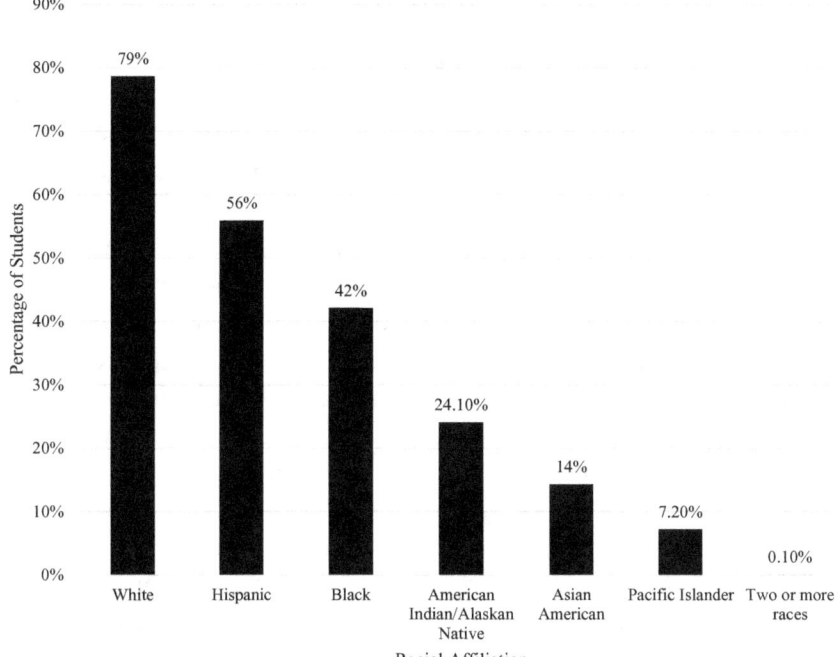

FIGURE 1.0 US Public School students tend to attend Institutions with students with matching racial and ethnic backgrounds

Note. Data presented above is from the Pew Research Center's analysis of data from the US Department of Education and the National Center for Educational Statistics (2020).

through a lens of improvement and growth, not personal fault. The comfortable, stable, status quo of my upbringing was no longer a pillow to protect my fall. While that felt challenging, I recognized it was necessary.

This internal awakening followed me as I left college and entered the teaching profession. With that feedback-prompted learning comes revised emotions as I reflect on my experience as a white student at a white school. The smile that comes to my face when thinking about my elementary school experience quickly fades as I consider the systemic implications of the racial dynamic of my schooling.

Teaching in the Familiar, in Unfamiliar Ways

After graduating with a BA in Education and Child Study and an MEd in Elementary Education, I was ready to have a classroom of my own. I landed at a tiny elementary school in western Massachusetts that was strangely familiar to the educational setting that I experienced as a student. The starkest similarity: it was a predominantly white school.

As I first began my job-search, I thought that the closer I could get to what I experienced as a student, the better the experience would be as a teacher. I had seen what it was like for some teachers in urban settings with a lack of resources and funding. I told myself that I wanted to teach where I could focus on my students, not the need for resources. A school like the one of my childhood seemed ideal as a teacher. Sounds pretty privileged, right?

Getting this first job offer felt like a golden opportunity. Initially, I was comforted by how familiar the school felt to me due to its alignment with my own experience. I thought, if I can't teach in my own hometown, this is the next best thing. As "woke" as I deemed myself, I was not ready to turn down the chance to work in a place of privilege. Remember I said that I was still learning?

It did not take long for my racial understanding from college to shake me from that place of complacency. When teaching social studies to my fifth-grade class, I was shocked to find over half the class was unfamiliar with the concept of enslavement. I was baffled. How could they have gone that long in life without discussing an ugly, but integral part of our nation's past? This was just the start. As I continued teaching, I became increasingly aware of how little attention was paid to Black, Indigenous, People of Color (BIPOC). I noticed students repeating their parents' beliefs or expressing ideas of their own accord that showed obvious biases and prejudice toward BIPOC. When trying to gauge colleagues' receptiveness to bringing multiculturalism into the school culture on a wider scale, I was saddened by the lack of support expressed from colleagues and administration. In sum, to discuss the whiteness of the school was to stir a pot that the majority did not want stirred. As motivated as I was to cause widespread change, I reflected on my own understandings. Before I could have wider change, I felt I needed to do some learning myself.

Increasing My Awareness

As I took advantage of trainings and resources on antiracism and anti-bias through local professional development providers and online platforms (Learning for Justice, Edutopia, etc.), I became increasingly aware of systemic inequities and the privileges that I held due to the color of my skin. For example, the fact that I have multiple grocery stores near my home for fresh produce, I can go for a walk without any fear for my safety, I can drive my car without worry of a police stop turning into a scene of brutality, are all testaments to the fact that I am a white woman who lives amongst other white people, mainly. These revelations were powerful, to say the least. As I made progress in understanding myself and my world more, I started to bring my antiracism motivation to my classroom.

While starting my doctorate, I turned to my own classroom domain to pursue racial conversations in a predominantly white student-teacher dynamic, since this was where I had the most control. The larger school community was not ready for this work, so I chose to refine my practice within the confines of my classroom. The literature lacked information about how to support a white educator teaching white elementary students about race, so I started keeping tabs on what I was doing and how things went. Endless online research and bookstore visits led me to materials that were related to teaching about race within this racial dynamic, but nothing "hit the nail on the head." Sure, I gleaned helpful insights from how to talk about race with white high school students and young students of color, but my actions were then tailored through my own understanding and interpretation. Since I did not have any resources that aligned with my scenario, my approaches were always with a sense of trepidation and doubt. I functioned through a system of "trial-and-error" since I did not have a resource that directly said an approach was recommended for white teachers teaching white elementary students. While the dearth of resources of my particular situation made the process of finding information more cumbersome, I did not let it stop me.

I made mistakes, had glorious moments of progress, and experienced both doubt and inspiration. The work was tiring and motivating all at once.

As I began tying my experiences into my doctoral research, looking at classroom-oriented resources, I was disappointed with the struggle I faced finding information related to my specific situation: A white teacher educating white elementary students about race. Particularly, I felt administrative support would be very helpful, but my research with the focus fell flat. In fact, this scarcity of information inspired my doctoral dissertation, which led to a book, titled, *Exploring the Role of the School Principal in Predominantly White Middle Schools: School Leadership to Promote Multicultural Understanding* (Boivin, 2020). I had interviewed principals at predominantly white, rural schools with middle grades (5–8) to learn about what principals could do to better support white teachers of white students when addressing race in the classroom.

As I neared the end of my doctorate, I decided that this was work I wanted to bring to teacher preparation programs.

Supporting Other Educators

As I write this book, I am an Assistant Professor of Elementary and Early Childhood Education. I have brought my unrelenting motivation to spread antiracism and equity in education in various forms in this role. For example, I am co-chair of my department's Anti-Racism Matters Committee and my college's Diversity and Equity Steering Committee. I also co-facilitate an antiracist book study for seniors and run another book club in the summer for faculty. My main role as a faculty member is to support undergraduate students in their trajectory toward becoming licensed educators in Massachusetts but have become increasingly interested in supporting colleagues on their journeys as well.

In my role, I frequently have white teacher candidates say to me, "Ideally, I'd like to teach in my hometown after graduating." When I inquire where that is, I often learn that it is a predominantly white school. In a nutshell, predominantly white schools will continue to remain in the US for the foreseeable future and the teaching profession continues to be predominantly white. The dynamic of white teachers teaching classes of white students is not going anywhere anytime soon.

The idea of a field guide for white teachers of white elementary students on how to teach about race popped into my head one day when preparing a lesson for a class I was teaching. I envisioned a book that is easy to read, approachable, and one that teachers could read before bed or keep on their desks for a quick glance. It could be used by students pursuing educator licensure or practicing teachers. It could inform administrators, educator preparation faculty, and more. Well, that's this book. This is the book that friends in the field have been asking me to write. This is the book that fills the literary void that has vexed me for years. This is the book to change many white students' experiences at school for the better.

Preparing Yourself for this Book

Maybe this is your first time reading a book about how to talk about race, or maybe you've read everything you can find and are always reaching for resources. Either way, I hope that this book reaffirms some ideas you may hold, challenges perspectives you may have, answers some questions about which you wonder, and inspires new queries that burn in your mind. I hope you read this book comforted by the fact that you are taking action and that you're not alone; there are others like you, who need help with how to talk about race with white elementary students, so you are not alone on this journey. I hope you also embrace the discomfort that is inherently a part of this work. Some approaches may appeal to you, whereas others may not. Just know, that in no way does this book advocate for making students, teachers or anyone, of any race, feel bad for the color of their skin.

As Beverly Daniel Tatum (2017) writes, there are four ways to be white, which include ignorant, colorblind, and racist.

She contends that schools can encourage students to create a fourth category of whiteness: the antiracist white identity. This book will help you on your journey toward an antiracist white identity and will support you as you encourage antiracist identities in your students.

More specifically, I aim for you to walk away from reading this book being able to:

- Articulate an understanding that white teachers teaching their white students about race can have future systemic benefits.
- Commit to self-work as a prerequisite to supporting students' racial learning while digging into the privileges of being a white teacher.
- Strategize ways to spread antiracism and racial equity throughout an entire school's culture via school community buy-in and support.
- Implement approaches to tie in race for each of the main academic subject areas.
- Cultivate new skills in how to talk to white elementary students about race, as a white teacher.

As you dive into this book, maybe you have a particular question in mind, or a subject area in which you hope to address race. This book can be read cover-to-cover or used as a reference. I encourage you to write on the pages, use a plethora of sticky notes, and get messy with the process. Chapters have reflective prompts that motivate contemplation and inspire action. These prompts can be redone over time to see how your answers change and gauge your growth. In sum, read this book as it suits you and your needs.

To give you a bit of a road map of the book, here is a summary for each chapter:

- Chapter 2: Racial Segregation in America's Schools Today
  - This chapter provides an overview of the previous and current pervasiveness of whiteness in the

teaching profession through statistics and facts. In addition, this chapter briefly looks at the history of the racial segregation of schools and connections to racial segregation of housing. I debunk the myth that racial segregation of schools is no longer present in the US. Lasting change requires systematic reform to take place, which has yet to happen. This chapter also addresses the idea that racial conversations as a white teacher in a white classroom is a step toward bringing greater awareness to systemic oppression faced by BIPOC individuals. This idea contends that the greater the number of white people, who inherently hold privilege, are aware and motivated to bring equity, the more likely it will be that they will eventually enact change. This approach, however, does not change the system directly or immediately. The impact these conversations about race can have on each student personally, and on society on a larger scale, is delineated. If antiracism could play a more prominent role in predominantly white schools, then maybe true systemic change is possible. This chapter concludes with self-reflective questions centering on the readers' understanding of systemic racism, digesting the segregation of schools and what it could take to integrate schools, and the important role of utilizing Critical Race Theory.

- Chapter 3: Helping Ourselves Before Helping Our Students
  - As teachers, we are inherently role models in many different ways. From what we eat, to what we wear, students often look at our actions through a lens of aspiration. How we talk about race and address our biases is no exception. This chapter discusses the importance of modeling this work to students and outlines recommendations white teachers can use to help address their biases in their personal

lives, to then transcend into their professional lives (DiAngelo, 2018; Oluo, 2018). The chapter provides vignettes that model self-reflection and actions related to diminishing biases. Ideas to place emphasis on thoughtful usage of skin color as a descriptor is unpacked. Race descriptors can be opportunities to embrace racial differences positively and normalize racial differences as part of society, but if not used carefully, it can center whiteness and/or perpetuate stereotypes of BIPOC. This chapter ends with reflective prompts that address the main ideas presented to encourage the reader to consider where they stand with their self-work.

- Chapter 4: The Importance of Support
  - This chapter delves into the role that school community "buy in" can have in spreading antiracism values throughout a school and entire district. I focus on how this work can start within a solitary classroom, but ideally will spread to a school-wide cultural norm. This includes other teachers, parents/caregivers, administration, and school stakeholders. Hopefully, as others start to see the powerful work a single teacher is doing, motivation will spread, thus leading to the school influencing the city/town where the school is located and maybe other schools in the district and beyond. In particular, I discuss the role that principals and superintendents play in making racial conversations more approachable in classrooms and as part of the school culture as a whole, and recommendations to administrators as to how they can support white teachers hosting racial conversations with white students (Boivin, 2020). Teachers who view these recommendations and feel these ideas/actions are lacking at their school will be encouraged to advocate for such supports. It is necessary that this chapter addresses the possible pushback that can occur when pursuing

this work and strategies as to how to handle it. This chapter ends with reflective prompts about their school community and actions they have taken and plan to take related to what is covered in this chapter.

♦ Chapter 5: Starting Small and Keeping It Real

  ♦ The previous chapter ignites a motivation to have an impact in a single classroom, as a way to evoke change on a larger scale. However, this work requires incremental steps and inherently demands a plethora of patience, similar to the self-work described in Chapter 2. While the subsequent three chapters are specific to particular academic areas, this chapter discusses the small moments that serve as opportunities to trying racial conversations. Such moments are chances to "dabble" in this meaningful work. These are gateway opportunities for teachers to try out the act of addressing race, before they are ready to take more explicit lesson-based approaches. This chapter shares how teachers can talk about the obvious: "We are all white, how can we achieve authentic understanding of racism in this context? We can't!" These steps then lead to digging deeper on a personal level with students (refer back to self-modeling) and unpacking their privileges. Recommendations for classroom guidelines for racial discussions, of which students have a say, are delineated. It is also important that parents/caregivers are aware that these conversations are taking place and are in no way a means to make children feel guilty for their whiteness. Recommendations for addressing resistive parents/caregivers is unpacked. The Learning for Justice Standards provide a useful structure for supporting this approach. I also discuss the importance of providing a safe space for students to digest current events tied to racism and tips for hosting those conversations. This chapter concludes with reflective questions that are scenario-based to think about opportunities to react constructively to students' questions and comments, and the ever-present media.

- Chapter 6: ELA Approaches
  - English Language Arts (ELA) is one of the more approachable subject areas to have students delve into exploring race and biases. Even when working with a boxed curriculum, there is room for providing students opportunities to read and write about race. This chapter talks about the power of self-expression through writing exercises and how literature can be used to offer perspective-sharing for students. The impact BIPOC representation within literature can have on students' decentering of whiteness is emphasized as well. Students should know that books about main characters who are BIPOC could be telling a story that is not focused on race. A variety of examples for grades 1–6 are supplied to show the approachability of addressing race and biases when working on ELA skills, all tied to the Common Core State Standards (CCSS). A fifth-grade example would be having students read and have discussions about the young-adult version of the book *I am Malala.* The story shows the adversity faced by a young girl in Pakistan who was shot for going to school and advocating for female education. Such a book unlocks the topic of prejudice against a particular group and opportunities for writing reflections on how prejudices are part of US culture and actions that can be done to diminish the oppression. At the second-grade level, the book *Race Cars: A Children's Book About White Privilege* can be used with second graders to think about what privileges come with being white. As students listen to a read-aloud of this book, they could answer prompting questions to identify the emotional experiences of the race

cars and later relate the story from white and black cars to white and black people. This chapter leads to reflective prompts regarding reading and writing as gateways for addressing race and bias.

- Chapter 7: Math and Science Approaches
    - In contrast to ELA, math and science are known to be far more quantitative and not popular venues for exploring race and biases. However, there is untapped potential here. For example, math standards (i.e., CCSS) focus on data analysis and provide opportunities to look at racial disparities and injustices in various communities. Math and science are subjects where whiteness as the norm can be challenged and displaced. Word problems about shopping can use food stamps or international currencies instead of dollars, the names of people in those problems can have more traditional names from other races and ethnicities, and recipes problems can be for dishes from other cultures. Avoiding every math problem being about Judy and Billy buying flour to bake a cake will expose students to a normalcy that is less rooted in whiteness. Science lessons can still be standards based, like with the Next Generation Science Standards (NGSS), yet still foster increased awareness of race. For example, racial biases could be explored in research when evaluating data. Math and science lessons are also opportunities for students to become increasingly aware of unequal representation of BIPOC people in these fields and consider the reasons why this has occurred. Reflective questions about using math and science as vehicles for racial exploration are supplied at the end of the chapter.
- Chapter 8: Social Studies/Civics Approaches
    - This chapter looks at how elementary social studies curricula provide a simplified, whitewashed version of US history and oversimplify the history

of enslavement and racial injustice (Kendi, 2016). Examples of narratives that glorify whiteness and ignore the "ugly" side of American history are explored. For example, while Thomas Jefferson, a prominent founding father in history, has been touted as a role-model figure, the fact that he enslaved people and likely fathered children with an enslaved woman, Sally Hemmings, has been disregarded from history. Powerful black figures have been disregarded or their stories have been incorrectly represented over time. Take Malcom X, for example. While a member of the nation of Islam, he touted violent ideologies toward white people, in the name of Black Power. However, after leaving the nation of Islam and traveling, his message changed to one of peace and equity. He has the potential to serve as a role-model of revising one's perspective for the better, publicly. Rather, he is still cast as a too-extreme activist in Martin Luther. King Jr.'s shadow. The importance of unpacking the true past is explained in this chapter as a means to not repeat history, which opens the door to make national progress toward equity. Civics education has been undermined due to overemphasis on ELA and science curricula in public schools, so cross-disciplinary approaches are explored as well. College, Career, and Civic Life (C3) Standards provide a foundation from which educators can craft these integrations. The chapter ends with social studies and civics-related questions to reflect on teaching practices that can be improved and new ideas for next steps. Such reflections may inspire educators to relearn the history they thought they knew with powerholders and whiteness decentered.

- Chapter 9: Social-Emotional Learning Approaches
  - Talking about race, biases, and social justice can be emotionally taxing and deemed as "touchy." This chapter provides recommendations for how

to ensure that students have a safe space to do such uncomfortable learning. Racial healing is a process (Singh, 2019). This chapter talks about building empathetic skills in white students when understanding experiences of people of other races and acknowledging the lack of understanding that inherently comes with this work because as white people, we will never truly understand what it is like to be a BIPOC person in America. Students can learn healthy, productive ways to express emotions on their journeys of antiracism. I address the emotional tax that this work can take on teachers and make self-care recommendations for them. A helpful framework to structure this Social-Emotional Learning (SEL) approach is through the Collaborative for Academic, Social, and Emotional Leaning (CASEL) Framework, which will be explored. The chapter ends with reflective questions about how teachers can care for their white students socially and emotionally in this work, as well as take care of themselves.

- Chapter 10: Continuing the Journey and Setting Goals
  - This chapter summarizes the book's major themes and recommendations. In addition, other resources and next steps are supplied to motivate the reader to continue this work and recognize that antiracist efforts must be never-ending; this work is lifelong. This final section concludes with goal-setting prompts to have readers write out their aims and actionable next steps.

This work is not as effective if done in solitude. As you read this book, refer to it in-action while in the classroom, and reflect on its contents, I encourage you to join an online community through Facebook. Search for the group titled, "White Teacher, White Students." You'll know it is the correct group because the group picture is the cover of this book. The group is intended for the readership who wants to continue the conversation, share ideas and experiences, ask questions, and support other white teachers of white elementary students. It is also a space where educators of color are more than welcome to support this work and provide useful insights and tips. When possible, I will weigh in as well.

The online community is a means to which you can continue this work and continue to evolve. While there is no summit to this mountain, and the climb can feel grueling, reflect on the impact you are having on our nation's future. Your role as a white teacher of white students is important.

And a note on language: the abbreviation, BIPOC is used throughout this book. There are flaws in this term, especially with how it centers Black and Ingenious within the category of People of Color without naming other marginalized groups (Deo, 2021) was coined by white folks—not including the input of those of whom the term is meant to represent (S. Garcia, 2020). BIPOC has been criticized as "lazy" and that saying black, Latine, etc. is preferred. I fully acknowledge that listing all marginalized groups throughout this book would be the most appropriate way to recognize those who face racial marginalization. In addition, I considered Global Majority as a phrase to use, but decided to reserve to use that term on a macro-scale when trying to highlight that whiteness is not the predominant race in the world. After thoughtful contemplation, I decided that the abbreviation of BIPOC would be used for ease of reading and for representing more than just black people, but I acknowledge the imperfections of this abbreviation.

Dr. McGowan Weighs In

Reading some of the terms in this chapter is a reminder that descriptors for different racial groups change over time. For example BIPOC compared to people of color where the term BIPOC is specifically acknowledging the historical and current racial challenges facing Black and Indigenous People. Other examples include slavery or enslavement and slave or enslaved person where the terms enslavement and enslaved person acknowledge the humanity of the Black people who were robbed of their freedom and human dignity. With this being stated, do not let the fear of using the wrong terms stop you from engaging in this important work of educating White children about the historical and current conditions surrounding race in our country. When mistakes are made regarding terms, learn from those mistakes, and keep moving on your journey toward gaining knowledge about how to effectively have these conversations in your classrooms.

References

Boivin, J. (2020). *Exploring the role of the school principal in predominantly white middle schools: School leadership to promote multicultural understanding*. Routledge.

Deo, M. E. (2021). Why BIPOC fails. *Virginia Law Review, 101*(117), 115–142. https://virginialawreview.org/articles/why-bipoc-fails/

DiAngelo, R. J. (2018). *White fragility: Why it's so hard for white people to talk about racism*. Beacon Press.

EdBuild (2019, Feb.). *23 billion*. EdBuild Report. https://edbuild.org/content/23-billion/full-report.pdf

García, E. (2020, Feb. 12). *Schools are still segregated, and black children are paying a price*. Economic Policy Institute. https://www.epi.org/publication/schools-are-still-segregated-and-black-children-are-paying-a-price/

Garcia, S. (2020, June 17). Where did BIPOC come from? *NY Times*. https://www.nytimes.com/article/what-is-bipoc.html

Green, M. (2018, Feb. 7). *Why are American public schools still so segregated?* KQED. https://www.kqed.org/lowdown/30098/why-have-americas-public-schools-gotten-more-racially-segregated

Kendi, I. X. (2016). *Stamped from the beginning : The definitive history of racist ideas in America*. Nation Books.

National Center for Educational Statistics (2020, Sept.). Race and ethnicity of public school teachers and their students. Data Point. https://nces.ed.gov/pubs2020/2020103/index.asp

Oluo, I. (2018). *So you want to talk about race* (1st ed.). Seal Press, Hachette Book Group.

Pew Research Center (2021, Dec. 14). *U.S. public school students tend to go to schools where their classmates share their racial and ethnic background*. Pew Research Center. https://www.pewresearch.org/short-reads/2021/12/15/u-s-public-school-students-often-go-to-schools-where-at-least-half-of-their-peers-are-the-same-race-or-ethnicity/ft_21-12-03_schoolrace_1-png/

Schaeffer, K. (2021, Dec. 15). *U.S. public school students often go to schools where at least half of their peers are the same race or ethnicity*. Pew Research Center. https://www.pewresearch.org/fact-tank/2021/12/15/u-s-public-school-students-often-go-to-schools-where-at-least-half-of-their-peers-are-the-same-race-or-ethnicity/

Singh, A. A. (2019). *The racial healing handbook: Practical activities to help you challenge privilege, confront systemic racism & engage in collective healing*. New Harbinger Publications, Inc.

Tatum, B. D. (2017). Why are all the black kids sitting together in the cafeteria?: And other conversations about race: Vol. 3 trade paperback edition; Twentieth anniversary edition. Basic Books.

2

Racial Segregation in America's Schools Today

The Whitewashed Field of Education

This chapter explores the historical racial segregation of America's schools and how it persists today. Ideas related to what enables the segregation to continue and policy-related ideas for systemic reform are touched upon. Having at least a surface-level understanding of the structures in place that allow predominantly white schools to exist and the steps that it could require for them to become extinct allows you, dear reader, to see that this is going to take a long time for us to see widespread change. You'll see a theme throughout this chapter that this work is going to require "generational change." The problem of systemic racism and the resulting segregated public schools cannot be solved with one single action or by one single person. This takes entire generations of people over generations of time. While I am hopeful that such change will happen, the ideas presented in later chapters of this book can help us in the meantime, while predominantly white schools are still commonly found in every state in the US. By working with the system that is in place, we can hope to change the system to be vastly different and integrated in the future.

Brown v. Board Was Not a Panacea for Systemic Racism Affecting Schools

History time! Stay with me here. Don't let your eyes glaze over or skip this part with the excuse, "I'm focused on the future, not the past." We have to do the work of reflecting on the past to see what we, as a nation, did wrong if we hope to do better in the future. This section provides a *brief* historical synopsis of the racial segregation of schools.

While widespread, deep-rooted, authentic racial equity in schools can and should happen in the US, it has never happened. Never. Not even after the Civil Rights Movement. To provide a quick overview of the racial segregation of US schools, let us begin in 1868 when the Federal Government ratified the Fourteenth Amendment to the Constitution (Library of Congress, n.d.-a). In this amendment, the civil rights of individuals, including African Americans, were protected against state encroachment. While this was a step forward, it was met with stark opposition. In 1896, the case of *Plessy v. Ferguson* centered around racial segregation on public transportation. The case was brought to Louisiana State Court, which decided to uphold racial segregation. "Separate but equal" was deemed constitutional. The Supreme Court denied an appeal to overturn the decision.

It was not until the 1930s that lawyers from the National Association for the Advancement of Colored People (NAACP) began planning their approach to argue that separate education was unconstitutional (Library of Congress, n.d.-b). They prioritized the notion that every student of every race deserves the best education possible. It was no secret that white schools offered more to students than black schools. From the quality of learning materials to the structural integrity of school buildings, black schools sadly paled in comparison to white schools. In June 1950, a well-respected attorney, Thurgood Marshall (later the first black Supreme Court Justice), met with the NAACP's board of directors (Library of Congress, n.d.-c). At that time, Marshall began to shift his prioritization away from racial inequality experienced in black schools versus white schools. Rather, he put his sights directly on the racial segregation of public education with the hope that desegregation would mean educational equality. The NAACP started pushing cases forward with this focus and then Oliver Brown's concerns about the distance his daughter had to walk to an all-black school made its way to the highest court. The case of *Brown v. Board of Education* involved four states (Kansas, South Carolina, Virginia, and Delaware) and the District of Columbia and Marshall served as the NAACP's chief counsel. On May 17, 1954, the court made racial segregation of schools illegal. The court provided a second opinion on the matter on May 31, 1955, which further confirmed the decision.

Many Americans were still greatly divided on the issue. Some Northerners and Southerners argued that the NAACP's work was rooted in communism (Library of Congress, n.d.-c). Marshall stated that he thought full desegregation, nationwide, would take up to five years (Rothstein, 2017a). He neither anticipated the heavy resistance nor did he and pro-desegregation supporters think that this would still be an issue today. Yet, here we are in terms of school's racial segregation, not much has changed. In fact, as of 2018–2019, one in six public school students attended schools where 90% of their classmates were of the same race (Roos, 2022). The ramifications for the teacher workforce are still felt today. After *Brown v. Board* was decided, there were massive layoffs for teachers of color: in the South alone, upwards of 38,000 black teachers lost their jobs and the teacher workforce has never recovered (Lash & Ratcliffe, 2014). Whiteness still overwhelmingly prevails in various stages of the teaching profession. From educator preparation enrollment to practicing teacher rates, teachers are predominantly white across the nation (US Department of Education, 2016). This disparity is even depicted in teacher retention rates, which are higher for white teachers than black and Latinx educators. The trend has been depicted over time. "The share of White teachers has decreased about 8 percentage points since the 1987–1988 school year (the earliest period with comparable data), when about 87% of teachers were White" (Schaeffer, 2021). However, the percentage of Latinx and Asian educators grew during that time period, but the percentage of black teachers declined.

Furthermore, the lack of new policies and expiration of older integration plans have led to the growing segregation between white students and students of color (Lockhart, 2019). The Northeast is where the most evident examples of segregation in schools take place (Roos, 2022). While people against the integration of schools caused harm and slowed the initial changes in response to the Supreme Court ruling, it was residential segregation that was hindering the process, and the US government was not helping.

The US government owns much of the blame for the persistent segregation of schools that the *Brown v. Board* decision could not fix. Policies to try and directly integrate schools have come and failed. Even in the north, which has commonly been seen as more racially progressive and proud of not contributing to Jim Crow norms, racial integration of schools has not gone smoothly. The "Boston Busing Crisis of 1974" is an example of how resistant many white people in the north have been to integration, even when transportation was supplied (Boston Research Center, 2018). The District Court of MA required full racial integration of students, and the result was massive protests and white parents pulling 30,000 white students out of Boston Public Schools and enrolling them elsewhere. Since the busing did not lead to fully racially integrated schools, in 1988, the Boston School Committee reinstituted the allowance of parents to simply send their children to neighborhood schools. These neighborhoods in Boston, however, were racially divided since the neighborhoods were racially divided. As of 2018, even though 54% of Bostonians reported themselves as white, a mere 14% of the students attending Boston Public Schools are white. More than half of the Boston Public Schools are racially segregated with 90% of enrolled students being of color. Simply, Boston Public Schools are more racially segregated than they were before the busing crisis occurred. The racist underbelly of Boston was fully exposed, and the city has yet to shake the reputation. Boston's busing crisis took an approach that lacked depth and consideration of the other systemic issues that play into the racial segregation of schools. The approach was fast but ineffective and its failure is still felt today.

Policy can do better and needs to do better if we are to expect deep-rooted, long-lasting racial integration. The next two sections unpack two facets of enacting such change: policy and social complexities. These two sections are not intended to provide a road map for change but rather are meant to articulate how multifaceted the solution needs to be, furthering the notion that *this is generational work.*

Changes Needed Part 1: Policy

The question remains: how can racial integration of schools be achieved without the backlash that Boston faced, especially in times of incredible racial tensions? Policy could play an important role, but research shows it would ideally need to focus on three central components of a vicious cycle. The three components are (1) residency, (2) income, and (3) school funding.

Integrated Residency

The Fair Housing Act of 1968 intended to prevent future discrimination in residential areas, but it lacked a focus on dismantling the residential segregation that was already established (Rothstein, 2017b). Public policy did nothing to stop discriminatory zoning, subsidies, taxation, redlining, and more, which all contributed to the racial residential divide that is starkly visible today. "White flight" to the suburbs has left urban residency mostly filled with people of color and the suburbs and rural towns filled with white folks. Zou and Cheryan (2022) write, "Whites perceive stereotypically foreign racial and ethnic minority groups—Latinos, Asian Americans, and Arab Americans—to pose a foreign cultural threat to their American culture and way of life" (p. 15). They add, "this perceived threat predicts Whites' living preferences and desires to leave residential neighborhoods with growing racial and ethnic minority populations" (Zou & Cheryan, 2022, p. 15). Evidently, "white flight" is alive and well.

Clearly, it was not "de facto" racial segregation that took over and persists today. Such a label would mean that the government is not held responsible for the racist property sales that took place. "De jure" is the more appropriate description, meaning that the government made this racial segregation possible. Once these norms were established, they have been further cemented over time. Public policy does nothing to prevent these norms from persisting and nothing to dismantle the divisions that have already been entrenched in society. Residences continue to be racially divided, meaning that neighborhood school enrollment continues to be racially divided. Such schools, filled with predominantly students of color, in turn, receive less funding (EdBuild, 2019). Simply put, better-resourced neighborhoods increase educational attainment (Turner & Gourevitch, 2017). It has been found that students in higher-quality K-3 classes earn more later in life and have increased college attendance rates by the time they turn 27 years old (Chetty et al., 2010).

Income Equality

Public policy has done little to achieve making income equality a realization. Until people of color are making comparable salaries to white people and can afford to live in the same neighborhoods, this residential conundrum will continue to mean schools are largely racially segregated in the US. Since salaries are greatly influenced by education, if students of color do not receive the same level of academics as white students, their future incomes will suffer. A successful high school degree or GED could lead a student onto higher education, thus increasing that person's odds for a higher salary upon degree completion. When looking at adults ages 25 and older, 15% of Hispanics and 23% of Black people hold a bachelor's degree (Patten, 2016). This is much lower than the 36% of white people and 53% of Asians. It's no secret that more education means a higher income and lower unemployment rates. Figures 2.0 and 2.1 depict just that.

Lesser quality of education is just one challenge faced by students of color, since they are also subject to discriminatory hiring practices and workplace discrimination that subsist. These are examples of social complexities that are discussed later. Even though people of color could make more money with a higher education degree than without one, gender and skin color will still affect incomes (Patten, 2016). Lower future incomes mean

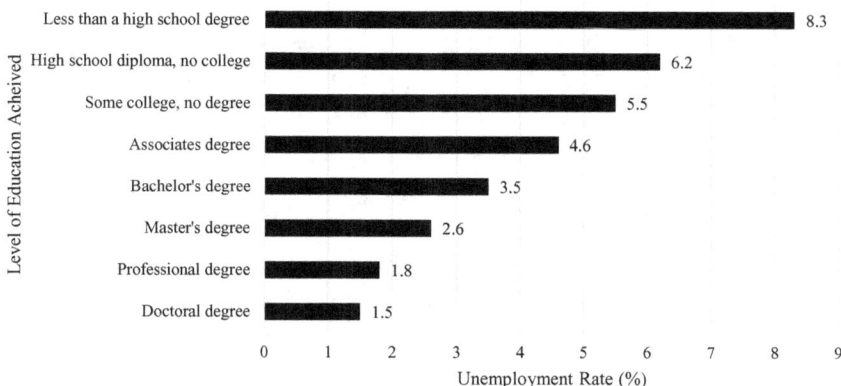

FIGURE 2.0 More education, lower unemployment (2021).
Note. Data presented above is from the US Bureau of Labor Statistics (2022).

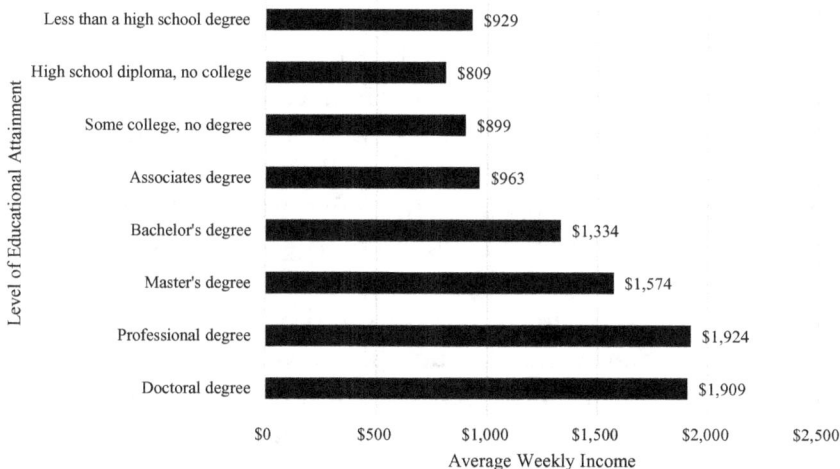

FIGURE 2.1 More education, more income (2021).
Note. Data presented above is from the US Bureau of Labor Statistics (2022).

many people of color will later only be able to afford to live within the same racial divides. In other words, the segregation cycle continues.

Equitable Funding for All Schools

To conceptualize the funding disparities among schools, it is necessary to look first at the mechanisms in place that determine how much money goes to which districts. A major problem within the US education system is how schools are funded. Property taxes typically determine a school's funding, which affects the resources and quality of teachers it attracts. During the 2018–2019 academic year, 45% of a school's funding comes locally, this can leave certain schools at a particular disadvantage (U.S. Census Bureau, 2021, as cited in Peter G. Peterson Foundation, 2021). Since local funding is largely based on property taxes, it means that a school's funding is 40% through property taxes, on average in the US (Peter G. Peterson Foundation, 2021).

A mere 8% of a school's funding is from the federal government, with the intention of supplementing state funding to support at-risk students (like Title I and special education). The remaining 47% comes from state funding, which is where it gets complicated. How do states determine how much money to give a school? In 45 of the 50 states, formulas control school funding and have ignited confusion, controversy, and legal battles (Urban Institute, 2017). While the formulas are intended to provide enough funding for every school district and increase financial equity, sometimes the formulas are not able to predict how districts allocate their funds based on various incentives. States use different funding models, each with their own pros and cons. While equity is kept in mind at the state level, it is not always achieved due to such heavy value placed on property taxes in determining a school's local funding. Even though a patchwork approach consisting "of complicated funding policies are supposed to level the playing field for all low-income students, they leave high-poverty nonwhite communities even further behind their high-poverty white peers" (EdBuild, 2019, p. 5). Whiteness is then associated with better education, wealth, and prosperous students with bright futures.

As a result of this dependence on local funding of our schools (largely fueled by property taxes), America is the only developed country in which students from wealthier families are the recipients of more education funding than their peers from low-income families (Ark, 2020). An overdependence on property taxes to fund schools propagates this segregation cycle.

The Vicious Cycle Explained

Now that we went over three central holes that policy could potentially fill, let's put it all together. The more education that a person receives, the more money they are likely to make. The greater the income, the more expensive the home. Pricier homes typically mean pricier neighborhoods and more property taxes funding the local schools. The more money a school receives, means better resources and higher quality teachers, thus increasing the quality of the education the students receive. The lower the quality of education a person receives, the less money they will likely make (especially if they don't go to college). The less they make, the cheaper the home they can afford. The cheaper the neighborhood, the fewer dollars going to the local public schools. The poorer the school, the lesser the quality of the education and the lower the future income for those students. Until this cycle ends, the racial inequities in education will prompt racialized income inequality and wealth gaps will perpetuate racially segregated residential areas.

As overly simplified as my description may be, the bottom line is that *education* is helping to maintain racial inequities and segregation, but *education* is the tool that could evoke deep-rooted change. Education is both the problem and the solution. Let's now dig a bit deeper into the facts and complexities of this vicious cycle.

Furthermore, schools with more money commonly rate higher academically and can have lower dropout rates. For example, a New York study found that the dropout rate went from 0.8% to 0.5% and funding increased from 2% to 3% (Lee & Polachek, 2018). A study out of Massachusetts found that increased funding was directly correlated to increased test scores (Nguyen-Hoang & Yinger, 2014). What matters most, is that the equitable funding is thoughtfully allocated (Jackson, 2020). More money is not the answer, rather, more purposeful money is the solution. However, until school funding is truly equitable, and not as dependent on property taxes, school options for students living in communities of predominantly people of color will be typically lower than the options for students living in communities of predominantly white people. Equitably funding schools filled with students of color would put an end to the notion that money follows white people. Granted, this is a very simplified breakdown of the systems corruptions, but its need for revision is still palpable.

While I could articulate ideas for what policies could make racially integrated neighborhoods more than just an ideal, that is not my intention. My goal is for you to consider the systems that have caused racial segregation of schools and maintain that segregation. I implore you to recognize the segregation and make others aware of it, especially at the legislative level. Maybe directly impacting integration is not the first step. Maybe the first step is ensuring every student in the US, regardless of race, has access to the same quality of education. Such a push could lead toward income equality and slowly shift the residencies of Americans to be more integrated.

With this policy-based approach to looking at how to solve the racial segregation of society and racial inequities, there are many social layers to this dilemma that mean that policy can only go so far. Social change needs to marry policy change for long-lasting integration and racial equity. As this policy section depicts avenues to raise the quality of education of students of color and give the skills and learning needed for higher income, it does not address the social complexities. What about the sense of belonging and shared culture forged in communities of color? Some argue that whiteness shouldn't need to be present in black communities and black people shouldn't need to be present in white communities for everyone to thrive equitably. While that idea certainly carries weight, it is important to not entrench ourselves in an acceptance that segregation can sustain without inequity. We, as a nation, have tried it before, but "separate but equal" didn't work, to say the least. Such a perspective should serve as a reminder that integration requires white people being mindful of their presence, privilege, and influence in spaces of predominantly people of color. The process requires white people listening, giving voice to people of color, making sacrifices so that historically marginalized people can thrive for a change. Policy does not immediately make an entire population change its perspective and become automatically racially inclusive. Social shifts paired with policy make for long-lasting change.

While policy has the power to be impactful, it is unrealistic to think that policies to end racial segregation in a deep-rooted, long-lasting, meaningful way could happen quickly, like within a single administration's term. Such legislative changes with a focus on racial equity will take lifetimes. *This is generational work.*

Changes Needed Part 2: Added Social Complexities

Societal motivation and buy-in can also carry out the legislative changes, even though resistance should be expected. However, looking beyond policy, everyday people can make changes in our society. Dismantling the segregation of public schools needs more than policy. Societal changes are an integral part of the process.

The Importance of Social Capital
While money was a huge ingredient in the policy section and a driving element to uplift minoritized groups in their societal standing, social capital is not addressed via the policy-only perspective. Money can only go so far for a black family and can mean much less for them if they live without interracial social capital amongst white people. Social capital is defined as the "concept in social science that involves the potential of individuals to secure benefits and invent solutions to problems through membership in social networks" (Poteyeva, 2016). Social capital can be broken into three layers. These include social connections, levels of trust in those relationships, and the resources and benefits that are given and taken in the relationship. Interracial social capital is the same process, but between people of different races.

When white people enslaved black people during the formative years of this nation, interracial social capital for black people suffered greatly. Enslaved peoples' lack of social capital was due to white people viewing people with darker skin as "sub-human." The relationship between an enslaved person and an enslaver was not one built on the three tenets of social capital, as described above. The lasting effects of white people not making interracial social capital possible has been detrimental to people of color in the US. Interracial social capital, or the lack thereof, has historically hindered people of color's ability to climb the socio-economic ladder *en masse* (Abbott & Reilly, 2019).

While white people have historically prevented interracial social capital from thriving, people of color have bonded together to forge social capital within their racial communities. The fact that people of color have resilient, strong social capital within their communities of color challenges the long-held assumption that people of color must have very low social capital (Averett, 2021). Social capital amongst people of color simply looks different than social capital amongst middle-class white people. As Averett (2021) explains, it is people of color who have needed a sense of community the most when battling against the societal oppression that they face. She adds that religion is marked as a major unifying outlet for many people of color and offers a venue to check in on one another and ensure everyone has what they need.

While social capital amongst people of color has been found to be incredibly strong and has shown to withstand through a global pandemic and horrific natural disasters (Averett, 2021), prejudice still drives whites wanting to withhold social capital from people of color in their communities. While people of color's social capital in spaces with white people have improved from the times of enslavement, racism persists and prevents many white people from valuing people of color equally. I think of examples of people of color with the financial means to send their children to elite private schools and get told by another parent, when not even asked, that the school offers financial aid. The white parent spoke out of the assumption that a person of color would need financial aid to attend such a school. I also think of workplace discrimination that prevents an equally or more qualified person of color from getting a promotion and seeing a white colleague get the job. The prejudice and stereotypes that white supremacy casts upon people of color inhibits people of color from being able to increase their social capital amongst white people. This can appear in even subtle ways. Munn (2018) saw a trend of a phenomenon called the "one friend rule" in which, "whites mobilize a 'close' interracial tie to project a generalized value for diversity while simultaneously limiting access to personal resources." Munn (2018) contends that this "rule" makes it much harder for people of color to gain and use social capital. Simply having interracial relationships doesn't always mean there is an equal exchange of social capital between the two parties. People in Munn's (2018) study showed how some white people can say they have a "close" relationship with someone of color to raise their status and appear as if they value diversity but do nothing to provide the person of color with any social capital. This has ramifications for people of color since social capital means social mobility (Abbott & Reilly, 2019). The "one friend rule" is a mechanism employed to hinder racial equity (Munn, 2018).

In a nation where interracial social capital is widely weak, more opportunities to forge authentic relationships amongst people of different races could be the tool needed to increase interracial social capital in the US population. This process of cultivating interracial relationships, that leads to interracial social capital, could begin in the public education system. Segregated schools may be only hurting the interracial social capital from existing. Stearns (2010) wrote that when high schools are racially segregated, those students are more likely to be racially isolated in the workforce ten years later. Workforce racial isolation is very troublesome because 80% of jobs are secured via personal or professional networking (Freeland Fisher, 2019). Racially segregated employment networks mean that people of color are not in the networks of higher-earning, white-collar positions, since those are largely in white networks (Brondolo et al., 2012). Residential and educational segregation limits the opportunities for people of different races to dismantle biases and stereotypes, thus racially isolating their social networks and maintaining societal segregation.

Building interracial social capital in our nation's children can start in different ways. This can look like white parents signing up their white children to play sports or participate in extracurricular activities in a more racially diverse area. As the organization Integrated Schools (2022) contends, when white parents have multiple neighborhood schools from which to choose, considering sending their white children to schools that are predominantly students of color can be impactful on interracial relations as well. Even if sending a white child to a school that is predominantly enrolled by students of color is not possible, the focus on intentionality in providing children with opportunities to forge meaningful relationships with people of different races can help normalize interracial relationships and diversify personal and professional networks, thus helping to dismantle segregation on many levels. It's important to keep in mind that when white parents integrate their children into spaces of predominantly people of color, it's integral that white parents know how to enter those spaces with respect, humility, and an open mind.

If interracial social capital is important for people of color to acquire social mobility and integrated schools can help facilitate that, why don't white parents start doing their part and all start sending their children to schools enrolled by mainly students of color? Oh, if only it were that simple.

A grass-roots effort to get white parents to send their students to schools that enroll predominantly students of color is valiant and there are groups trying to promote that movement. However, there are many hurdles that keep white parents from delving into this effort. White parents can feel unable to send their white children to a more racially diverse school for a myriad of reasons that include, but are not limited to the following:

1. Convenience (common thinking: "The school is not located as close to my home.")
2. Home price and taxes (common thinking: "I paid a lot of money for my home for my children to attend highly rated schools nearby and continue to pay taxes to support those schools.")
3. Stereotyping (common thinking: "Going with a more diverse school means that I would sacrifice academics for my child.")

4. Reputation (common thinking: "I saw online that the school got a low ranking.")
5. Resources (common thinking: "I want my child to have access to advanced classes and lots of extracurriculars that aren't offered at those schools.")
6. Not fitting in (common thinking: "My white child will stick out at that school for being white and that will have social ramifications.")

While white parents may see great value in their child being around people of various races, the justifications listed above prevent many of them from sending their children to schools that are predominantly students of color. An argument may be, "Well, if white parents aren't willing, why don't parents of children of color start sending their children to predominantly white schools?" There are many facets of that argument that are unsettling. Many of the same justifications reappear for parents of color. For example, the predominantly white schools are usually not as conveniently located. In US history, whiteness has always been centered and prioritized. People of color have historically had to sacrifice to get what they deserve. Why would it be okay for parents of students of color to sacrifice convenience and potentially subject their child to feeling racially out-of-place when white parents are not willing to do that same? Furthermore, it is often not even logistically possible for parents of color to send their children to predominantly white schools due to time and financial constraints. Schools other than the one located right in the neighborhood are often the only option for parents of color.

Convincing white parents to integrate their white children into spaces of predominantly children of color will not cause integration right away since white parent buy-in is low, due to the white schools still carrying the acclaim of being "the good schools." *This is generational work.*

Battling White Supremacy

While having opportunities to be around people of color and build relationships with them can be a powerful tool for white people to dismantle biases and address racism, white supremacy can subsist. White supremacy can be inaccurately portrayed as only consisting of extremists, like white nationalist hate groups that promote ideas like "white identity should be the organizing principle of the countries that make up Western civilization" (Southern Poverty Law Center [SPLC], 2021). These groups want to see whiteness be the majority Western societies. They see immigration as threatening their power and fear whiteness becoming the eventual minority race. White supremacy, in a more inclusive sense, includes anyone who feels as though they are better than a person of another race. A white supremacist does not need to be a member of a white nationalist group or even be explicitly racist. A white supremacist could uphold unconscious racism and consistently portray microaggressions.

Even if not part of one of these extremist groups, there are a concerning number of white Americans who feel as though their own rights and privileges are under attack when racial equity is even discussed. Due to the deeply polarized nature of that notion in recent years, Republicans and Democrats have been type-cast on opposing ends of fighting for racial equity. The stereotype of having to be Democratic to be in favor of racial equity and have racial conversations in the classroom has meant that Republicans want the opposite: no racial conversations in school. What extremes without any nuance! Such opposing views have led to debates regarding if Critical Race Theory should be addressed in schools. In this debate, CRT has been improperly characterized as teaching white students to feel guilty about being white (more on CRT in the next section). Politics has gotten in the way of truly considering how race can be discussed and addressed in schools and continues to obstruct our nation from having meaningful conversations that could help promote racial equity.

Aside from politics, parents with deep-seeded racism influence their children. Those children internalize the morals and ideals from their households and can bring those into school. Research has shown that, "parents play an important role in shaping children's values and their attitudes toward members of other ethnic groups" (Pirchio et al., 2018, p. 1). Even if a student is learning about racial equity at school and has students of color in their classes, the influence of parental prejudice can have on that student should not be discredited. For parenting to instill antiracist qualities means a societal shift needs to occur to normalize that practice as much as we normalize teaching "good manners."

I am not going to pretend I have an answer for how to abolish white supremacy and white nationalism. Those ideas took a long time to develop with many factors at play to gain steam, meaning they will take a long time with many approaches to dismantle. As daunting as that may be, I firmly believe that if children are raised and educated with a consistent antiracist mentality, they will influence future generations, and the racist societal norms of modern-day will slowly begin to fade. Did I mention… *this is generational work*?

White Classrooms with White Teachers: Let's Start Some Generational Work

I don't know about you, but after digesting how racial segregation was established, fought, and remains a palpable issue today can make my stomach turn. As a white person, sometimes I feel like it's too big of a problem to undertake because there are so many layers. I mean, policy changes to affect residency, income, and school funding? Mix in all those social complexities of white supremacy, political partisanship, social capital barriers, and white supremacy and we have one ugly mess.

Having grown up in a predominantly white town and currently living in a predominantly white town, and the schools have been and continue to be predominantly white in both of those places, I had a glimmer of hope. If a majority of white parents are going to continue to send their white children to white schools and be taught by white teachers, then the system remains the same. However, what if those students no longer see those spaces as the real world? What if they wake up to the racial segregation of which they are a part? What if they start seeing the color of their skin, their whiteness, as a source of privilege? What if they started learning about what it means to be an antiracist and care about the lives of people of color, even if not present in their learning environment? What if white students recognize their voices can carry weight toward raising the voices of people of color? What if our white students in white schools help enact *generational change?*

Critical Race Theory may be able to make those questions reasonable to consider as a possibility. CRT, as loaded as the title has become due to misnomers about it, could be an integral tool in the effort of enacting generational change of racial equity. CRT may be deemed controversial because it forces us to see injustices that white privilege often blinds white people from seeing. As Bell (1995) states, "Critical Race Theory recognizes that revolutionizing a culture begins with the radical assessment of it." CRT is a critical assessment of systemic racism that is pervasively throughout the US. Kimberle Crenshaw (2021), makes clear that attacking CRT is a poorly veiled attempt to preserve white supremacy and maintain a whitewashed view of history and modern life.

Gloria Ladson-Billings describes CRT as a legal framework that contends that racism is an embedded facet of the legal system and our nation's policies. According to Ladson-Billings' CRT definition, racism is not solely a result of individuals' biases (NPR, 2021). Ladson-Billings' has applied this lens to the field of education to explore the inequities in the education system and their ramifications (Ladson-Billings, 2021). Fox News anchor, Christopher Rufo, of the show, "Tucker Carlson Tonight" called on then-president Donald Trump to ban CRT in American schools and the then-president did just that. Fox News was perpetuating the misnomer that CRT was teaching white children to feel bad about being white. Even Ladson-Billings remarked that she couldn't find anything in the literature about saying one race is better than another. There is simply no presence of that idea or sentiment in the CRT framework. CRT has become a catch-all phrase for demonizing talking about race with children because it risks changing a system that has privileged white people. CRT isn't intended to be a curriculum in schools. When applied to education, it can be a lens through which we see institutional racism causing students of color to face disproportionately higher suspension rates, a lack of access to higher-level classes, higher assignments to special education, and more, all because of an educational system with racism running through its veins. With this in mind, maybe CRT can have a place in classrooms.

Maybe this framework from graduate studies in law school could influence elementary students. Why not? Why can't young students start to recognize that there are systems structured in ways to benefit some, but not others? Why not inspire them to recognize privilege and think about their roles for the future?

Until every white parent is willing to send their child to a school that is not predominantly white and until predominantly white schools are extinct, white teachers will need to know how to talk about race with their predominantly white classes. Even some of the most antiracist, "woke" white parents feel it could be too much of a sacrifice to not send their children to the "good white schools" because they want what's "best" for their children. Plain. And simple, these schools aren't going anywhere for a very long time.

Is a book about white teachers teaching white children about race just saying that these types of learning environments are okay? No, not in the least. What I'm arguing is that white teachers who are willing to have conversations about race and make antiracism a core learning objective in their classrooms can play a major role in this *generational work*. That's where you come in, dear reader. As a white teacher of a predominantly white class of students you have the opportunity to mobilize systemic change. You have the power to inspire future generations of white people to see the inequities and consider the complex solutions. You have the influence to motivate our nation's white citizens of the future to not be okay with the racial segregation of schools and other racial inequities. The greater the number of white people, who inherently hold privilege, are cognizant of their privilege and are motivated to promote equity, the more likely it will be that they will eventually enact change. Let's use these predominantly white spaces, where learning is the priority, to carry the message that the future is largely in our students' small, white hands. They can use those hands to either opportunity-hoard as much as their white privilege allows, or they can choose to enter the world striving to hold tight to hands of color and raise them high and strong. Let's encourage our students to notice the role their skin color plays in our nation's systems and how their learning environments are not reflective of our nation.

It is my honest hope that one day this book is *not* useful because predominantly white schools don't exist anymore. I dream of true integration of our schools, filled with equity and promise for every student of all races. But, since predominantly white schools are here today, and there's no sign that they will be extinct any time in the near future, we must use that venue to have racial conversations to inspire the *generational work*.

Reflective Questions

Take a walk, maybe stress-eat some chocolate, possibly let out a good cry, or scream into a pillow. It's okay to feel emotionally drained after facing the systemic realities head-on. That was a lot to digest in this chapter. When you're ready, come back to this section and reflect on the following questions:

1. What new ideas came up that surprised you? Did your white privilege blind you from any aspect of the realities presented?
2. What problems (policy-related, socially related, or both) made you feel like, "this work seems really hard"?
3. How are you seeing your role of contributing to generational work in your personal life? For example, are there actions you could take to build interracial social capital that doesn't fall into the "one friend rule"?
4. How would you describe the perception of CRT where you teach? Have you ever reflected on your school system through a CRT lens to notice systemic inequities? Try it can write notes on what you notice.
5. How are you honestly feeling about your role as a white teacher of white students when it comes to contributing to the generational work of racial equity?

Dr. McGowan Weighs In

The information provided in this chapter reminds me of the Ghanaian term, Sankofa which means we must learn from the past, as we work in the present, to prepare for the future. In applying the tenets of Sankofa to school segregation, this chapter provides a candid snapshot of past practices that have manifested into our present segregated school systems. Applying CRT can be a powerful framework for how we use what we have learned from the past and the present to construct a better future for all public school students.

References

Abbott, M., & Reilly, A. (2019, May). The role of social capital in supporting economic mobility. Office of the Assistant Secretary for Planning and Evaluation at the US Department of Health and Human Services. https://aspe.hhs.gov/sites/default/files/private/aspe-files/261791/socialcapitalsupportingeconomicmobility.pdf

Ark, T. V. (2020, Oct. 6). The biggest source of inequity might be the way we fund our schools. *Forbes.* https://www.forbes.com/sites/tomvanderark/2020/10/06/the-biggest-source-of-inequity-might-be-the-way-we-fund-schools/?sh=640413c46b2f

Averett, N. (2021, Oct. 1). Social capital in black communities is often overlooked. *Scientific American.* https://www.scientificamerican.com/article/social-capital-in-black-communities-is-often-overlooked/

Bell, D. A. (1995). Who's afraid of critical race theory? *University of Illinois Law Review, 1995*(4), 893–910.

Boston Research Center (2018). *Desegregation busing.* https://bostonresearchcenter.org/projects_files/eob/single-entry-busing.html

Brondolo, E., Libretti, M., Rivera, L., & Walsemann, K. M. (2012). Racism and social capital: The implications for social and physical well-being. *The Society for the Psychological Study of Social Issues, 68*(2), 358–384.

Chetty, R., Friedman, J. N., Hilger, N., Saez, E., Whitmore Schanzenbach, D., & Yagan, D. (2010). How does your kindergarten classroom affect your earnings? Evidence from Project STAR. *Quarterly Journal of Economics, 126*(4), 1593–1660.

Crenshaw, K. (2021, July 2). The panic over critical race theory is an attempt to whitewash U.S. history. *Washington Post*. https://link.gale.com/apps/doc/A667224360/GIC?u=mlin_s_bridcoll&sid=ebsco&xid=fdf91358

EdBuild (2019, Feb.). *23 billion*. EdBuild Report. https://edbuild.org/content/23-billion/full-report.pdf

Freeland Fisher, J. (2019, Dec. 27). How to get a job often comes down to one elite personal asset, and many people still don't realize it. *CNBC*. https://www.cnbc.com/2019/12/27/how-to-get-a-job-often-comes-down-to-one-elite-personal-asset.html

Integrated Schools (2022). *About us*. https://integratedschools.org/about/

Jackson, C. K. (2020). Does school spending matter? The new literature on an old question. *An Equal Start: Policy and Practice to Promote Equality of Opportunity for Children*. https://works.bepress.com/c_kirabo_jackson/38/

Ladson-Billings, G. (2021). *Critical race theory in education: A scholar's journey*. Teachers College Press.

Lash, M. & Ratcliffe, M. (2014). The journey of an African American teacher before and after Brown v. Board of Education. *The Journal of Negro Education*, *83*(3), 327–337. https://doi.org/10.7709/jnegroeducation.83.3.0327

Lee, K., & Polachek, S. W. (2018) Do school budgets matter? The effect of budget referenda on student dropout rates. *Education Economics*, *26*(2), 129–144. https://doi.org/10.1080/09645292.2017.1404966

Library of Congress (n.d.-a). *A century of racial segregation, 1849–1950*. https://www.loc.gov/exhibits/brown/brown-segregation.html

Library of Congress (n.d.-b). *School segregation and integration*. https://www.loc.gov/collections/civil-rights-history-project/articles-and-essays/school-segregation-and-integration/

Library of Congress (n.d.-c). *Brown v. board at fifty: With an even hand*. https://www.loc.gov/exhibits/brown/brown-brown.html

Lockhart, P. R. (2019, May 10). 65 years after Brown v. Board of Education, school segregation is getting worse. *Vox*. https://www.vox.com/identities/2019/5/10/18566052/school-segregation-brown-board-education-report

Munn, C. W. (2018). The one friend rule: Race and social capital in an interracial network. *Social Problems*, *65*(4), 473–490.

Nguyen-Hoang, P., & Yinger, J. (2014). Education finance reform, local behavior, and student performance in Massachusetts. *Journal of Education Finance*, *39*(4), 297–322. https://www.muse.jhu.edu/article/546723

NPR (2021, June 6). *How critical race theory went from Harvard Law to Fox News*. https://www.npr.org/transcripts/1012696188

Patten, E. (2016, Jul. 1). *Racial, gender wage gapes persist in US despite some progress*. Pew Research Center. https://www.pewresearch.org/fact-tank/2016/07/01/racial-gender-wage-gaps-persist-in-u-s-despite-some-progress/

Peter G. Peterson Foundation (2021, Jul 14). *How is K-12 education funded?* https://www.pgpf.org/budget-basics/how-is-k-12-education-funded

Pirchio, S., Passiatore, Y., Panno, A., Maricchiolo, F., & Carrus, G. (2018). A chip off the old block: Parents' subtle ethnic prejudice predicts children's implicit prejudice. *Frontiers in Psychology*, *9*, 1–9. https://doi-org.libserv-prd.bridgew.edu/10.3389/fpsyg.2018.00110

Poteyeva, M. (2016, May 16). *Social capital*. Britannica. https://www.britannica.com/topic/social-capital

Roos, M. (2022, May 17). School segregation still common 68 years after Brown v. Board Report. *Newsweek*. https://www.newsweek.com/school-segregation-still-common-68-years-after-brown-v-board-report-1707588

Rothstein, R. (2017a, May 16). *Brown v. Board is 63 years old. Was the Supreme Court's school desegregation ruling a failure?* The Economic Policy Institute. https://www.epi.org/blog/brown-v-board-is-63-years-old-was-the-supreme-courts-school-desegregation-ruling-a-failure/#:~:text=Sixty%2Dthree%20years%20ago%20on,were%20half%20a%20century%20ago.

Rothstein, R. (2017b). *The color of law: A forgotten history of how our government segregated America.* Liveright.

Schaeffer, K. (2021, Dec. 10). *America's public school teachers are far less racially and ethnically diverse than their students*. Pew Research Center. https://www.pewresearch.org/fact-tank/2021/12/10/americas-public-school-teachers-are-far-less-racially-and-ethnically-diverse-than-their-students/

Southern Poverty Law Center (2021). *White nationalist*. https://www.splcenter.org/fighting-hate/extremist-files/ideology/white-nationalist

Stearns, E. (2010). Long-term correlates of high school racial composition: Perpetuation theory reexamined. *Teachers College Record*, *112*(6), 1654–1678. https://doi.org/10.1177/016146811011200604

Turner, M. A., & Gourevitch, R. (2017). *How neighborhoods affect the social and economic mobility of their residents*. US Partnership on Mobility from Poverty. https://www.urban.org/sites/default/files/publication/92956/how-neighborhoods-affect-the-social-and-economic-mobility-of-their-residents_0.pdf

Urban Institute (2017, Nov. 29). *How do school funding formulas work?* https://apps.urban.org/features/funding-formulas/

US Bureau of Labor Statistics (2022). *Education pays, 2021*. https://www.bls.gov/careeroutlook/2022/data-on-display/education-pays.htm

US Department of Education (2016). *The state of racial diversity in the educator workforce*. https://www2.ed.gov/rschstat/eval/highered/racial-diversity/state-racial-diversity-workforce.pdf

Zou, L. X., & Cheryan, S. (2022). Diversifying neighborhoods and schools engender perceptions of foreign cultural threat among white Americans. *Journal of Experimental Psychology: General*, *151*(5), 1115–1131. https://doi-org.libserv-prd.bridgew.edu/10.1037/xge0001115.supp

3

Helping Ourselves Before Helping Our Students

Grass Is Green, Sky Is Blue, and People Are White, Right?

As a white teacher, have you had to think about your race much throughout your life? I've had conversations with friends and colleagues about this and I have found that more often than not, white people do not really think about their race routinely, whereas people of color do. Granted, those conversations were mainly before the summer of 2020 and recognizing race is a bit more common. However, when I think about describing my identity, whiteness has never been a top descriptor, until more recently. I'm actually not alone in that. The Pew Research Center (2019) reports that only 15% of white people saw their race as extremely or very important to how they think of themselves. In contrast, 74% of black people said it was extremely or very important to how they think of themselves. The results for Hispanics and Asians were 59% and 56%, respectively.

Why don't white people think about their race? Well, it might be because it rarely puts obstacles in our way and American culture advertises and popularizes white imagery so much, that whiteness doesn't seem like anything special, just the norm. Once I started thinking more critically about this, it made sense. For example, when growing up, when someone described an object as "skin color," I would assume it meant a light beige. I never had a second thought of a band-aid matching my pale complexion. When watching shows like *Friends* or *Seinfeld*, I never thought ill of the fact that the central recurring roles were all white. Such normalization meant white acceptance and pervasiveness at a societal level. Why would I think of whiteness as central to my identity when the world around me depicts whiteness as nothing special, just the baseline norm. As a white woman in this society, it is understandable that I'd be more likely to link my identity with what sets me apart and makes me different because to claim whiteness as an identifier wouldn't seem special in a white-centric, westernized world.

Such a level of acceptance and normalization comes with vast privilege. As a white person, I inherently hold privilege in society, which allows me the luxury of not being oppressed because of the color of my skin. Black, Indigenous, People of Color (BIPOC), in contrast, may not want to have to think about their race routinely, but societal oppression forces them to think about the role their skin color plays in everyday life. For example, shopping at a store or driving on the freeway are different experiences for white people and BIPOC. A white person may be carefree and focused on their list at the store and get lost in a song on the radio when driving. In contrast, a BIPOC may notice shopkeeper stares and even get followed by an employee out of suspicion of shoplifting when at the store. A BIPOC may white-knuckle the steering wheel when passing a police car out of fear of being pulled over and risk facing police brutality. Two people, living in the same country, doing the same activities, can have very different experiences due to the difference of their race. As a white person, I have lived a life of perpetuating oppression unconsciously. Peggy McIntosh (1990) described white privilege as, "an invisible package of unearned assets which I can count on cashing in each day, but about which I was 'meant' to remain oblivious" (p. 31). She continues, "White privilege is like an invisible weightless knapsack of special provisions, maps, passports, codebooks, visas, clothes, tools and blank checks" (p. 31). It took me a long time to get to the point where I noticed the different lived experiences between white people and BIPOC. I attribute much of that to the fact that I was a white girl growing up in a white town with white parents and teachers who didn't speak about race often. When race was discussed, it was more in recognition or history, like learning about the Civil Rights Movement or Black History Month. In the predominantly white society in which I lived, racism was part of history, not the present, so we felt we didn't need to think much about race if it didn't affect us. I can recall our whiteness being so ignored that our school chorus, a group of all-white sixth graders, sang the song once sung by enslaved people called, "Pick a Bale of Cotton." I cringe at just the thought of this now. By not talking about whiteness, I didn't know that there was privilege in the color of my skin, and I was blind to the oppression BIPOC were facing. I lived in a white bubble, shielded by ignorance.

Developing a CRT lens for the world, I started noticing how race literally affects everything. Race plays a role in the clothes I wear, the house in which I live, the people in my social network, the food I eat, the shows I watch, and more. Race, a man-made construct, has infiltrated western society pervasively. The idea of race was created to manifest a hierarchy, with whiteness at the top. Race has nothing to do with biology, rather focuses on how people see themselves and each other (Brooks, 2019). Race first came about in the mid-17th century to justify enslaving Africans for forced labor in the American colonies (Bournea, 2021). From the establishment and continuation of enslavement, all the way through the Civil Rights Movement, racism served as a defining characteristic of America. But, societal structures, as discussed in Chapter 2, helped maintain those norms after the Civil Rights Movement. It is not reasonable to think that something that took so long to establish could be quickly or easily dismantled.

While I lived in racial ignorance in the white bubble that was my hometown and didn't think about race often at all, a CRT lens put the world into a whole new light for me. I have found that as a white person, once I started noticing the role of race in everyday life, it was hard to switch off. The fact that I went so long not noticing race in everything, however, speaks to the privilege embedded in my whiteness.

While some assumptions are true, like the grass being green and the sky being blue, assuming whiteness as the default race is simply an inaccurate way to describe an ever-diversifying nation. Predominantly white spaces need to start acknowledging how what their race means.

Role-Modeling for Future Generations

Breaking through the "white bubble" where I lived and routinely being around BIPOC was somewhat of a culture shock for me. I was overwhelmed by people who didn't look like me and classes that spoke about race and challenged the power of whiteness. It was the first time I started self-reflecting and noticing my biases. My CRT lens was first starting to take form. Now, this is at 18 years old and to be truthful, even as I write this book I feel I have a long way to go. I feel myself grappling with the first 18 years of my life and can't help but wonder where I'd be on my racial justice journey if I grew up talking more about race.

I think back to singing songs of the enslaved in chorus without a single peep about how wrong it was for 40-plus white kids singing it. I think back to the children's books that talked about MLK ending racism in the US, like the world I was experiencing was the "happily-ever-after" for America. I think back and can't help but wonder, "What if my learning experiences were different?" Even though my parents brought us to a neighboring city to play sports to meet people of different backgrounds and races, that was once or twice a week for brief sports seasons. I never had a role model who would openly express and model what it is like to be a white person who cares about racism in modern society. Some of the most prominent role models of my youth were my teachers and not even one of them modeled for me how to think critically about my skin color and my role in dismantling racism.

Teachers were for me, and are for many students, prominent role models. As teachers, we may not recognize the awesome power and influence we have as role models for our students. The food we pack for lunch, the shoes we wear, and the way we handle our emotions are all aspects of our lives that students notice and internalize. How we talk about race and address our biases is no exception.

As you're reading this chapter you may be wondering, "Okay, so I must have to model this work for students, but how do I do that?" My answer is that you wouldn't go into showing someone how to plant a garden if you've never done it yourself before, right? Well, this is similar. You wouldn't jump into modeling antiracism and decentering your whiteness in front of students if you haven't practiced, right? So that's what this next section is all about. We will unpack practices to do to address your own biases and recognize your white privilege before you can truly dive into working with students on these issues. As educators, we can look at this as (1) personal growth and (2) professional growth.

Personal Growth

Looking in the mirror to uncover and analyze our biases can be the epitome of uncomfortable for a lot of us. Who likes to hunt for and focus on imperfections? That's no fun. As a white person, it is easy to look at the idea of personal growth and be intimidated and try to avoid it. Evading the work is pretty easy since our society provides us comforts and privileges. To challenge our perceptions about race makes us question if we really deserve what we have. I'm here to recognize that you, by reading this book, are doing something challenging that you're choosing to face. Go you!

The subsequent subsection articulates some steps you can take on your journey toward being an antiracist white person. However, the strategies are not exhaustive, so I encourage you to explore the cited sources from this chapter to continue learning after reading this book.

Defining Your Past, Present, and Future

A useful first step is taking the time to write about your upbringing and personal history and the role race played and/or didn't play in your experiences. How does that all influence your current social status, education, relationships, employment, etc.? Thinking about the past can help illuminate what surrounds you and influences you today. Has anything changed? What has remained the same?

Looking at our past and present to spur change can start with looking at areas of improvement. There are anecdotes from my own reflections that spurred action as I transitioned from a non-racist to an antiracist (Kendi, 2019). For example, I noticed that my friend group had always been predominantly white and remained that way until recently. At first, I came up with excuses like, well that is just who went to my school or lived around me. Then, I challenged myself to consider the work that I was avoiding. I admitted to myself that if I wanted BIPOC friends, I could have some, but it would require effort. I'd have to actively seek opportunities to mingle outside of my immediate community. That work, however, seemed worth it. Now, I can say that I have truly increased the racial diversity of my friendships. Those relationships have been incredibly meaningful to me and teach me more than any book or podcast could about being a racially just person.

People around me, whether they be neighbors, classmates, family, and friends, have used racism as a source for joke-telling or the root of gossip. When racist jokes were told, I'd hear follow-ups like, "It's just a joke, I'm not racist or anything." When a new family moved into town, if they were BIPOC, I'd hear judgmental comments and concerns about the well-being and safety of the town. Similar instances have occurred in which I'd hear white people thinking that putting their racism in the form of an ill-humored joke or in gossiping whispers somehow made the racism less real or impactful. Rather than quietly presenting I didn't hear it or going along with it out of fear of fitting in, I openly challenge these exchanges. Sometimes it's in the form of "calling in" when I pull the person aside and talk about how their actions were far from okay (DiAngelo, 2018). Other times, it feels necessary to "call out" the person in front of others so that everyone can know that what happened is racist and not okay. Sure, my outspokenness has cost me some friendships and being in the white spaces where that rhetoric occurs is not as easy for me anymore. However, I take solace in the fact that when I enter those spaces now, people know that if I'm there, they shouldn't say racist things. If that means that there are fewer instances where racism is deemed accessible because of me, I feel I've made a difference.

What we absorb in the media can influence our perspectives powerfully. In fact, a survey found that 91% of Americans believe that media influences society and 75% of those surveyed believe that the ways that black people are portrayed in the media affect wider perceptions in everyday life (Alexander, 2020). While I was growing up, predominantly white shows were routinely on the television and my musical preferences were mainstream white artists. Even the books I read focused on white protagonists. I noticed that as an adult, even though the television shows, musical artists, and books that I consumed all changed, their whitewashed nature remained. With the rise of technology, the more pervasive media has become. I feared that my dependence on technology and the algorithms learning my preferences were causing me to be surrounded by more whiteness than ever before. Simply put, more content could mean more *white* content. I wondered if I could use technology to my advantage and go in the other direction. What if technology could help me diversify my media consumption to benefit my perspective? I'm proud to say that I've made great gains with this effort. All on my phone, I have access to endless music, videos, literature, and social media influencers. While it is easier than ever to selectively surround myself with whiteness, I've used technology to explore diverse music, books, podcasts, social media influencers, and more. I think that social media has been a powerful tool on my journey of becoming an antiracist because I have been able to join virtual communities of like-minded people who prioritize the voices of BIPOC. I fully acknowledge that people can also have completely opposite experiences where racism can overtake their social media feeds, but it does have the power to do good. Again, breaking my white-centric habits posed challenges and felt uncomfortable. It took more of my attention and thoughtfulness to be selective of the media I absorbed and to break my habits of watching the same shows and listening to the same music. The effort has been more than worth it because I have learned so much through media that decenters whiteness.

Identifying our privileges and biases and exposing ourselves to diversity should involve an intersectional lens. There are seven main areas that we can identify as identity layers that provide us with a privilege status or an oppression status (Singh, 2019). The social identity layers/systems of oppression include the following:

1. Race
2. Disability/ableism
3. Sexual orientation
4. Gender/sexism
5. Religion
6. Age
7. Social class

Keep these identity layers in mind on your equity journey, as intersectionality is a powerful aspect of this work.

Talking and Listening: The Power of Words and Being Okay with Mistakes

What we choose to say and when we choose to talk are two powerful decisions a white person can take, especially on a journey toward antiracism. At the start of this journey, I found it helpful to be less vocal as a starting point. As I was working on learning the correct terminology pertaining to racial justice and unraveling some long-held beliefs that were buried in white-privileged perspectives, I needed time to formulate ideas inside of myself before I was ready to articulate them. As I quietly learned and entertained internal dialogue, I realized that when I was ready to speak up, it would need to be different depending on the space in which I was entering.

Listening: As a white woman, entering predominantly white spaces feels comfortable for me and I feel as though I can be direct and forceful when needed. But does that approach work when I enter racially diverse spaces with a mission of antiracism? I then considered my role as a white person seeking to enter these unfamiliar spaces. As a person who has never faced racism, is it appropriate for me to tell BIPOC how to handle the racism problem in the US? I realized that entering spaces in which I am the racial minority, even if I am in those spaces to support racial equity, needs a different approach from me than when I was in white settings. First and foremost, I need to prioritize listening. Listening means that I am taking the time to learn from others and see what they need. Listening shows that I'm here and ready to be directed as to how I can be of best service. Listening communicates respect and gives other voices rise (Roberts, 2020).

In white spaces, if I felt I knew how to help, I was used to simply entering the space and sharing my ideas and what I thought was right from the get-go. In racially diverse spaces, I needed to recognize that I was there to support others, not direct people. Otherwise, I would risk trying to serve as a "white savior" or be displaying "performative allyship." These are ways that white people take actions that they claim are for the betterment of others but truly are for their own moral and social profit. As Nova Reid (2021) writes, black people don't need white people to rescue them. She says, "We have been rescuing ourselves and revolting against the oppressor throughout history" and adds, "What we really need is white people to do is consciously, consistently and intentionally unlearn racism." This process involves listening, responding, rather than reacting, and sees everyday racism and addresses it.

Thoughtful words: Oluo (2019) writes, "Too often whites at discussions on race decide for themselves what will be discussed, what they will hear, what they will learn. And it is their space." Speaking passionately without thought can be dangerous, especially as a white person. As a white woman used to speaking her opinions, I sometimes come off as overly confident and comfortable in my knowledge. When it comes to talking about race, if I ever feel 100% comfortable with what I am saying I'm doing something wrong. Why? Because I can never be 100% comfortable talking about racism when I've never experienced it myself. If I aim to raise the voices of BIPOC and not seek "white saviorism," then I need to bring humility with me. I must recognize that my whiteness carries privilege and I've been afforded opportunities and social status due to my skin color, not due to merit. As a white person, I recognize that showing up and listening comes first. Waiting to talk, after I've taken the time to learn, is an important step before I can contribute. I also need to avoid half-listening and then going straight into action, because that spurs performative allyship (Reid, 2021).

Being thoughtful with my words has also impacted my personal conversations in very casual settings. I have come to realize that using skin color as a descriptor when talking about people is complex. I have, on countless occasions, been watching a movie or show and described a white character by their occupation, hair, color, or clothing. When describing a person of color, I routinely have just said things like, "the black lady or man." I had to step back and notice how my descriptions were normalizing/centering whiteness in this situation. To point out a character was black was further emphasizing that it is what differentiated the character from the norm.

In contrast, using race as a descriptor can be an opportunity to embrace racial differences and highlight how someone's race can be an asset and carry great, powerful, positive significance. In a nation where many people tiptoe around race in conversation, normalizing race in conversation can be a tool to encourage conversations about race and maybe even address inequities. While talking about all races routinely can be helpful, if not centering whiteness, it is important that the way we talk about certain races is not paired with stereotypes. For example, if someone always pairs "black" with crime, then the stereotype of black men being criminals is perpetuated, which we've seen has had disturbing societal ramifications. How we talk about race can have powerful ramifications on how children talk about race (Belli, 2020). Race descriptors can be opportunities to embrace racial differences positively and normalize racial differences as part of society, but if not used carefully, it can center whiteness and/or perpetuate stereotypes of BIPOC.

Professional Growth

I am a firm believer that it is necessary to grow personally before attempting to grow professionally, since our professional growth is dependent on our personal growth. In fact, studies have shown that personal motivation to be antiracist can help individuals continue this work, even when it gets challenging (Ivey-Colson & Turner, 2020). Our professional growth as educators has direct effects on others and a strong, foundational base personally can help situate each of us up for success. I like to think of professional growth as an educator within three central domains: working with students, working with colleagues, and working with the school community. While these domains do not fully address every person with whom you will work, it makes for a helpful framework for self-accountability.

Working with Students

As previously mentioned, as educators, we are powerful role models for our students, like it or not. We wield an influence on them at paramount times of development. Such influence cannot be taken lightly, which you obviously are not taking lightly because you are reading this book. There are some simple tactics to try that involve showcasing your personal growth to students. These include naming biases, embracing mistakes, not running from racial questions and conversations, and embracing race and equity work in all academic disciplines.

Naming biases: Working with students on their biases and understanding race starts with modeling your personal growth. Simple actions are explaining how you discovered a once implicit bias (self-analysis tools or implicit bias test) and explaining how you are focusing on this area to learn more, which shows that you are proactive and reflective. Verbalizing stereotypes that you once believed and explaining what you did to enhance your perspective to dismantle those stereotypes in your head is an impactful approach. For example, when reading the book *The Name Jar* to students, which is a book about a Korean girl in America who wants to change her name because American classmates cannot pronounce it properly, I might share that I once thought of all Asian cultures as the same. I previously thought that Chinese, Japanese, and Korean cultures were all the same because I thought people from these countries all looked the same. That is very incorrect, as each of these countries has unique cultures, customs, and traditions. I could share how now I have been working to read books and watch documentaries to learn how these countries vary. By naming your biases and working on them routinely, you are also diminishing implicit biases that can manifest nonverbally. Nonverbal cues can communicate biases, which young children have been found to internalize and can manifest as biases that they later hold (Suttie, 2017).

Embrace the mistakes: Openly sharing the self-improvements that we are making as people humanizes us to our students and provides opportunities to make mistakes and talk about the mistakes with students. I might share how I said something wrong before and am working on it, when helping students change the language that they are using. For example, I might hear a student accuse another student of "Indian giving," which is an old saying that refers to people who give gifts and then ask for them back later. This inappropriately has been associated with Native Americans being thieves, as described in Thomas P. Slaughter's book, *Exploring Lewis and Clark: Reflections on Men and* Wilderness (Schilling, 2018). While it is easier to pretend we didn't hear that or we can simply brush it off as "kids will be kids," addressing this with students is like how we address these situations in our personal lives: we kindly, and gently, investigate language that is biased or stigmatizing.

Don't run from race: Not shying away from questions or conversations about race shows that you care deeply about the topic and that it is valid for students to ask questions and have conversations related to race. Avoiding the topic communicates that conversations about race have no value (Harrison, 2020; Seitz, 2020). When I taught fifth grade, I remember a white student asking me if that means his black friend would have been a slave in early America. I regret to say that I was early on my racial journey and brushed off the question by saying something like, "We don't want to think like that because those were old times" as I quickly proceeded onto my lesson. I think back to my response with repulsion because I had, in front of me, on a silver platter, the opportunity to talk to my students about how far we've come as a nation and how far we have to go. While pursuing such an approach would have required me to carefully not center the one Black student in my class, it would have been a chance to validate my student's desire to talk about race while raising awareness about racial disparities that still exist. This includes ensuring that our history is taught through a lens of truth and a commitment to not omit the "ugly." As described by the Zinn Education Project (2022), "The more clearly we see the past, the more clearly we'll see the present—and be equipped to improve it." Embracing an ugly past could prevent an ugly future.

Race in all the disciplines: While most of us do not have a designated time block on our class schedules for racial conversations (we wish!), these approaches can be worked into our instruction seamlessly and sometimes even subtly. The subsequent chapters of this book are divided by subject area so that together, we can unpack addressing race and equity by academic discipline. By embracing racial conversations and explorations in all academic disciplines, we model the pervasiveness of race and how it affects all aspects of life. You, as the teacher, are then modeling that there is no part of your day together that doesn't warrant some attention to race, just like how no part of our everyday lives is free from the influences of systemic racism.

Working with Colleagues

Like the work that we do in our personal lives, not everyone who surrounds us will be as motivated to do this work. Even so, that doesn't mean we shouldn't try to open some racial conversations and efforts with colleagues.

Finding like-minded colleagues: Forging and maintaining a community of like-minded people has been an important facet of racial equity work from its beginning. The Civil Rights Movement would never have happened without a strong sense of community among similarly passionate people. The same goes for the Black Lives Matter Movement. While solo self-improvements, as explained earlier, are incredibly important, so is working alongside other like-minded colleagues (Detert & Roberts, 2020). Since racial equity work can get unfairly politicized in various spaces, some colleagues at your school or within your district may feel shy about speaking up about how much they care about this work. Finding colleagues who would make great teammates may be as easy as joining an already-formed racial equity committee. However, in contrast, some of you may need to do more purposeful searching for these people. One idea is to talk to your administrator about your passions and see if they know who may be willing to connect. Alternatively, you can set up a casual afterschool "snacks and conversation" group about racial equity and see who comes. I have found my teacher's union to be a great place to connect with similarly motivated educators. Finding those like-minded colleagues can help you gain confidence in your efforts and help with supporting others on their racial journeys as well.

Grade-level/department planning: Your grade-level or department team may feel like you "click" on lesson planning, and unit scope and sequencing, but you may not "click" when it comes to social justice integrations. This can be a "squishy" topic that feels unapproachable to many and sticking with the mandated curriculum may be the focus of team meetings. Even if you feel like you're still new to this work, making it known that you want to do more in your curricula is a great starting point. Starting simple with sharing what you're doing in your domain and sharing materials you have already created and prepared takes out an intimidating step for your colleagues, which makes implementation more realistic and approachable. Sharing what you are doing within your own classroom, while highlighting how you are still addressing your district's curricular requirements, says to colleagues, "if I can do it, you can do it." Such sharing may encourage others to want to try on their own, share afterward, and maybe, the team planning time will evolve into race and equity-minded practices. Race and equity could shift from a sidenote to the meat of the meeting.

Faculty/staff meetings: Faculty and staff meetings can be long meetings with lots to address. Often, they take place after a draining school day and let's face it, using that time to talk about uncomfortable topics, like racism, is not very appealing as a participant, nor as the person to speak up because racial conversations can be exhausting and as we've addressed previously and super uncomfortable. However, this is one of the few times where there is a captive audience of all faculty, and a face-to-face meeting makes it harder to ignore the topic of race than it is to ignore an email. This is a prime opportunity to first talk to your administrator to get on the agenda. When making such a request, I recommend meeting with your administrator about what you'd like to talk about and see if they can support you. Having their backing can make a huge difference. I recommend one of the following topics as a starting point to make racism a focus at your predominantly white school:

1. Let's form a group of faculty dedicated to antiracism and hosting racial conversations in our classrooms to strategize.
2. I'd like to share the ways that I have been addressing race in my class and would be eager to learn what others are doing (then share an online repository, like a Google Doc. or Padlet).
3. Offer ideas related to addressing race within agenda items that are already being covered. For example, if revising the school's mission statement is on the agenda, maybe inquire about racial justice.

It's important to note that when bringing up a desire to address race in a space filled with white people, the majority of whom are not especially motivated in this work, there may be some pushback, which is very important to anticipate ahead of time (Deter & Roberts, 2020). Inclusive framing to diminish defensiveness with an emphasis on togetherness can inspire collective progress. This is why administrator support is so important. If your administrator does not feel inclined to support you, it is important to not give up. Sometimes it takes presenting your motivation and desire for more racial work in your school to know who is ready to partner with you, even if only one or two people. And at times, you may feel like the only one. I've been there and it's scary. My greatest recommendation is to truly own your classroom space and have confidence that others will come around. It just may take time.

Working with the School Community

Schools can often function as microcosms of society, which can be good in the sense they prepare students in ways that prepare them to contribute as citizens when adults (Sackstein, 2015). However, schools can be microcosms of the negative aspects of society as well. Societal biases creep into schools, like white people's propensity to embrace colorblindness, for example (Will, 2020). White schools, in turn, can feel self-insulated in a way that means the outside world, with its push toward racial justice and emphasis on racial diversity can feel distant and unimportant. If schools reflect society, then a shift in schools could mean a shift for society and school-community relationships can be useful in this effort.

It's imperative to remember that outside of the school walls lays a larger community that may be able to support you in this work. Sometimes we need financial resources to improve classroom materials/curricula, other times we need restrictions lifted to have the freedom to talk about race openly in our classrooms. The school community is a great place to search for support, including, but not limited to, your families, the school committee, local officials, local businesses, higher education institutions, and activist groups/social justice organizations. As applies to contacting all community-based bodies in this section, it doesn't hurt to reach out, share your passions, and ask for support.

Families: Working with families in your efforts can help move your antiracist focus into students' home lives. This starts with strong lines of communication and resource-sharing (Learning for Justice, 2021). Parents may have connections and resources to share with you that are unexpected. All you need to do is share your initiative and ask. See what happens!

School committee/board: While school committee meetings "taking on CRT" have blanketed news headlines since fall 2020 (Kingkade et al., 2021), school committee's influence on what happens within schools can be quite impactful. Having conversations with school committee members about your concerns about feeling supported in having conversations about race and equity in your classroom and why such work is important could unlock school-wide support.

Local officials: People elected to local office tend to have a solid sense of the city/town's racial climate. They can make powerful allies in supporting you in your classroom work or even in your work trying to influence your school/district. Local officials are well-networked and can help put you in touch with like-minded people who may be able to help you. Attending city/town meetings can allow you to mingle with others as well as hear other perspectives. These meetings can even be a place where youth can have a voice, which is a teaching opportunity (Girl Scouts, n.d.).

Local businesses: Especially after the summer 2020 racial reckoning that took place after the murder of Breonna Taylor and George Floyd, many businesses released statements showing solidarity in the fight for racial equity and striving to do better. What better way to enact that desire than to help local teachers? It's time for businesses to be held accountable for the letters of commitment that they wrote in 2020 (Roberts & Grayson, 2021). Talking to local bookstores about donating multicultural texts, raising funds for guest speakers, and field trips from stores, restaurants, and services are all avenues by which you can encourage local businesses to put their solidarity into action or more boldly, "put their money where their mouth is."

Higher education institutions: As a professor in an educator preparation program, service to the community is part of my job. With many educator preparation programs trying to increase their capacity to teach future teachers about how to integrate ideas about race and equity into their teaching (Eddie, 2021), classroom teachers who are eager to do this work make stellar partners for us college faculty. By reaching out to educator preparation programs in your area, you may be able to support prepracticum students or a student-teacher in this work and they may even teach you some approaches, too! Also, the teacher preparation program you attended may not have taught you much about hosting racial conversations, particularly with white students, so asking local preparation programs for advice and resources is a great starting place. Not to mention, it further connects you with more like-minded people—did I mention the power of community in this work?

Activist groups and social justice organizations: Since community is foundational to racial equity work, reaching out to groups and organizations focused on racial equity and social justice can lead to more networking and resources. These organizations have impacted me both personally and professionally. For example, Educators for Anti-Racism is a group that focuses on supporting educators in bringing racial equity to the classroom. I attended their free, virtual conference in the summer of 2022, and I took so many notes from the brilliant speakers' sessions. The Zinn Education Project is another group with useful resources for teaching a more inclusive, truthful past.

This chapter is just a small snippet of the work that it takes to be antiracist personally and professionally. It's a lifelong journey that will not end for anyone. Constant learning and an understanding that it's ongoing are integral to your journey.

Reflective Questions

I now invite you to reflect on the ideas presented in this particularly uncomfortable chapter.

1. Can you summarize the work you've done to grow *personally* when it comes to racial understanding?
2. What areas warrant more attention/support?
3. What are your next steps for each of the areas you identified?
4. What supports/resources will you access to help you?
5. Can you summarize the work you've done to grow *professionally* when it comes to racial understanding?
6. What areas warrant more attention/support?
7. What are your next steps for each of the areas you identified?
8. What supports/resources will you access to help you?

Dr. McGowan Weighs In

As you think about the seven social identities outlined in this chapter, also consider how racial hierarchy impacts disability, sexual orientation, gender, religion, age, and social class. For example, the Women's Suffrage Movement was primarily focused on the needs of upper-class white women. Susan B. Anthony and Elizabeth Cady Stanton made it clear that they were working on securing the vote for white women. It was left to African American women's rights activists such as Sojourner Truth to fight for equality for Black women.

References

Alexander, B. (2020, Sept. 17). Two in three black Americans don't see themselves represented in movies and TV, study says. *USA Today*. https://www.usatoday.com/story/entertainment/movies/2020/09/17/study-black-americans-no-representation-movies-tv/3476650001/

Belli, B. (2020, June 15). It's never too early to talk with children about race. *Yale News*.

Bournea, C. (2021, Oct. 21). 'Race' is an invented concept, but an impactful one, researchers say. Ohio State News. https://news.osu.edu/race-is-an-invented-concept-but-an-impactful-one-researchers-say/

Brooks, M. (2019). Skin is a social construct. *New Statesman*, *148*(5475), 30–33.

Detert, J., & Roberts, L. (2020, July 16). How to call out racial injustice at work. *Harvard Business Review*. https://hbr.org/2020/07/how-to-call-out-racial-injustice-at-work

DiAngelo, R. J. (2018). *White fragility: Why it's so hard for white people to talk about racism*. Beacon Press.

Eddie, A. (2021). Unlearn: Preparing preservice teachers as antiracist educators. *Northwest Journal of Teacher Education*, *16*(2). https://doi.org/10.15760/nwjte.2021.16.2.11

Girl Scouts (n.d.). *The new cool girl hangout? City council meetings*. https://www.girlscouts.org/en/raising-girls/leadership/civic-action/guide-to-city-council-meetings.html

Harrison, R. R. (2020, June). *Talking to kids about race and racism.* Kids Health. https://kidshealth.org/en/parents/talk-about-race.html

Ivey-Colson, K., & Turner, L. (2020, Sept. 8). 10 keys to everyday anti-racism. *Greater Good Magazine.* https://greatergood.berkeley.edu/article/item/ten_keys_to_everyday_anti_racism

Kendi, I. X. (2019). *How to be an antiracist.* One World.

Kingkade, T., Zadrizny, B., & Collins, B. (2021, June 15). Critical race theory battle invades school boards—with help from conservative groups. *NBC News.* https://www.nbcnews.com/news/us-news/critical-race-theory-invades-school-boards-help-conservative-groups-n1270794

Learning for Justice (2021). *Critical practices for anti-bias education.* https://www.learningforjustice.org/sites/default/files/2021-11/LFJ-2111-Critical-Practices-for-Anti-bias-Ed-November-2021-11172021.pdf

McIntosh, P. (1990). White privilege: Unpacking the invisible knapsack. *Independent School, 49*(2), 31.

Oluo, I. (2019, Mar. 28). Confronting racism is not about the needs and feelings of white people. *The Guardian.* https://www.theguardian.com/commentisfree/2019/mar/28/confronting-racism-is-not-about-the-needs-and-feelings-of-white-people

Pew Research Center (2019, May 2). *Blacks are more likely than other groups to see their race or ethnicity as central to their identity.* https://www.pewresearch.org/race-and-ethnicity/2022/04/14/race-is-central-to-identity-for-black-americans-and-affects-how-they-connect-with-each-other/re_2022-04-14_black-identity_0-01-png/

Reid, N. (2021, Sept. 19). No more white saviors, thanks: How to be a true anti-racist ally. *The Guardian.* https://www.theguardian.com/world/2021/sep/19/no-more-white-saviours-thanks-how-to-be-a-true-anti-racist-ally

Roberts, L. M., & Grayson, M. (2021, June 1). Business must be accountable for their promises on racial justice. *Harvard Business Review.* https://hbr.org/2021/06/businesses-must-be-accountable-for-their-promises-on-racial-justice

Roberts, M. (2020, June 3). The best white statement to make right now may be to shut up and listen. *The Washington Post.* https://www.washingtonpost.com/opinions/2020/06/03/best-white-statement-may-be-shut-up-listen/

Sackstein, S. (2015, June 14). If school is not 'the real world,' what is it? *EducationWeek.* https://www.edweek.org/teaching-learning/opinion-if-school-is-not-the-real-world-what-is-it/2015/06

Schilling, V. (2018, Sept. 13). What or who is an Indian giver? A history of the offensive term. *Indian Country Today.* https://ictnews.org/archive/what-or-who-is-an-indian-giver-a-history-of-the-offensive-term

Seitz, N. (2020, Oct. 7). The benefits of teaching children to see race. *PBS.* https://www.pbs.org/parents/thrive/the-benefits-of-teaching-children-to-see-race

Singh, A. A. (2019). The racial healing handbook: Practical activities to help you challenge privilege, confront systemic racism & engage in collective healing. New Harbinger Publications, Inc.

Suttie, J. (2017, Jan. 31). How adults communicate bias to children. *Greater Good Magazine.* https://greatergood.berkeley.edu/article/item/how_adults_communicate_bias_to_children#:~:text=The%20results%20suggest%20that%20negative,to%20form%20their%20own%20biases

Will, M. (2020, June 9). Teachers are as racially biased as everybody else, study shows. *EducationWeek.* https://www.edweek.org/teaching-learning/teachers-are-as-racially-biased-as-everybody-else-study-shows/2020/06

Zinn Education Project (2022). *Why teach "people's history"?* https://www.zinnedproject.org /why/

4

The Importance of Support

Feeling Like the "Odd Activist Duck"

As a white person in a predominantly white setting, challenging the status quo can feel like "risk-taking." It can feel uncomfortable, tiring, and even threatening. As a new, young, white teacher at a predominantly white elementary school, I could sense the frustration and dislike that other teachers felt when I tried to spread antiracism and multicultural values/experiences to the greater school community. As soon as I attempted to share my thoughts outside my own classroom walls, I felt belittled and disrespected, like my message and moral mission for the sake of our students' development seemed trivial in comparison to upholding the whitewashed, Eurocentric norms that long preceded my hiring date. In a flock of mallards, I felt like the "odd activist duck."

I looked inward and took control of the learning environment that was my own domain. I focused on the 20 or so students I had the honor to influence and support 180 days per year. I took risks in my own classroom and encouraged my students to do the same. With a giant sign reading, "Make Mistakes!" high on the wall at the front of the room, I continuously pointed to those words to encourage my students to push their comfort zones and see what happens.

To help support me throughout my own mistake-making journey, which is inherently part of any journey involving racial conversations and exploring privilege, was my dear friend and colleague. I found my co-conspirator. We worked together to share plans and ideas for bringing antiracism and multiculturalism into our lessons. We talked about our struggles and times of doubt, our moments of feeling like our efforts were paying off, and our shared hope for our students' futures to understand their whiteness and privilege. I felt lucky I had a partner in this work, and I learned so much from her, especially when it came to texts to use with my students to spur such powerful conversations about race and equity.

As I focused on my influence in my own classroom, I had to wonder what it is like at similar schools to my own. At the time, I was pursuing my PhD as I taught full-time and decided to shape my dissertation in a way that I could learn more. I wondered if I could learn what principals could do to support teachers like me, who are white, teaching in predominantly white schools, and strive to cultivate antiracist future citizens who embrace all sorts of cultures and differences.

Principals, You Can Do More

As explained earlier, finding co-conspirators and allies in this work is a huge part of spreading the mission of racial discussions and exploration, leading to antiracist values for everyone in the school, especially the students. However, administrative support can play a huge role in this process (Boivin, 2020). I conducted a study for my doctoral dissertation that explored three questions:

1. To what degree do principals consider it a priority to expand multicultural understandings in predominantly white, rural, middle school grades?
2. What do principals report they are doing to expand multicultural understandings in predominantly white, rural, middle school grades?

3. What do principals report are factors and conditions that inhibit and support their efforts to expand multicultural understandings in predominantly white, rural, middle school grades? (Boivin, 2020, p. 46)

These guiding research questions were explored through a survey and follow-up interviews with principals across MA. They needed to work at schools that qualified as "rural" and contained the middle grades (5–8). The study yielded findings that have helped me think critically about how important it is to have a principal support a white teacher who wants to explore race in a predominantly white learning environment. The data allowed me to synthesize the findings into a succinct list of recommendations for principals if they were to successfully support teachers in this important work. The only revision that I would make to these recommendations is the usage of "multicultural understandings," which I would replace with "antiracism." I think that the phrase "multicultural understandings" is missing the important message of embracing racial conversations and unpacking privileges. As Endi Lee (Miner, 1991) described in an interview with Rethinking Schools, "a lot of multicultural education hasn't looked at discrimination" and that means it takes a superficial lens, as she describes in the Canadian education system as an example. If antiracist education is done well, it captures a variety of culture's perspectives and has whiteness take up less space, rather than other cultures' presence being in addition to the white superiority (Miner, 1991). Multiculturalism can be a stepping stone to getting to antiracism, but it is integral that it is not an end goal. Moving forward, as I refer to such recommendations, I will revise the language accordingly. The recommendations are as follows:

1. Include multiculturalism directly in the school mission.
2. Share personal multicultural understandings to benefit teachers and students.
3. Tie professional practice goals to the district or school improvement plans when the focus is on expanding multicultural understandings.

4. Provide more multicultural professional development opportunities to teachers.
5. Provide teachers with resources and time to practice modeling multicultural understandings for their students.
6. Take time to look at the school culture as a whole and consider how the culture embodies multiculturalism.
7. Help teachers plan how to use the required standards to leverage multicultural understandings in their curricula (Boivin, 2020, p. 133).

Are you a principal? Are you a teacher or parent with a good rapport with your school's principal? Are you a superintendent supporting a team of principals? If you could answer "yes" to any of those questions, then I urge you to share that list with them or consider its influence on your practice if you are a principal. If the list overwhelms you, that's normal. It's a lot to reflect upon, especially when requiring so much meaningful, widespread, deep-rooted action. I fully acknowledge that principals have an incredibly underappreciated, taxing, challenging position. The recommendation list is not meant to serve as a "to-do list" that one accomplishes in a week, a month, or even a single academic year. The recommendation list is meant to help administrators reflect upon areas of improvement and think about ways to take steps forward. If I were to highlight one recommendation as a powerful focus that truly connects to all the other recommendations, it would be, "Take time to look at the school culture as a whole and consider how the culture embodies multiculturalism" (Boivin, 2020, p. 133) but repositioned with antiracism as the goal.

The Power of School Culture
I left this study feeling personally hopeful. As an educator who felt a lack of support when trying to bring antiracism and the process of unpacking white privilege in her school, I thought of how powerful it would have been to my experience if I felt the school culture embraced these ideas. Just the thought makes me daydream as to what our all-school events would have been like. How our department meetings could have had such a strong

social justice orientation? How our professional development could have been so much more meaningful?

The largest takeaway from this study, for me, was the power of school culture. I appreciated how all-encompassing and powerful a school culture can be and how it could be the glue that holds together a community focused on a shared mission. I realized that the true epitome of support was in the form of school culture.

Once a school culture embraces an idea, it becomes part of the status quo and embodied values. The school culture shapes the goals of the district, schools, administration, and teachers. The school culture can be felt the moment a person walks through the front doors. It can influence the way a classroom functions, the atmosphere on the playground and cafeteria, and offerings outside of school hours. School culture can shape the physical space where learning, socializing, and creativity thrive. School culture can influence the formal rhetoric used in school notices and the informal discussions in the teachers' lounge. In essence, school culture that embraces understanding race and privilege is one that has the potential to support students, faculty, and administration that do the same. School culture can be toxic and hinder such positive strides toward equitable understanding, but we will focus on its positive possibilities with a motivation toward authentic change.

Strategies for Revamping a School's Culture

As Scribner et al. (1999) assert, a school's culture can center around a shared goal. To make progress toward a shared goal, it means that self-reflection needs to occur routinely. In short, if the shared goal of a school's culture revolves around discussing race and exploring privilege, self-reflection by community members on these topics will need to happen if progress is to occur. As explained in Chapter 3, self-reflection is a huge component of developing antiracism. Self-reflection can then lead to collaboration, which DeAngelo (2018) denotes as a necessary facet of addressing racism and biases. Scribner et al. (1999) agree that collaboration is a powerful tool in establishing a school culture. Without collaboration, progress is hindered or even stops.

Gay (1994) contends that a school's culture can be negatively influenced by biases and a school culture that makes students feel unwelcome or experience inequities can be connected to decreased student academic success.

Based on the list of principal recommendations, it's clear that improving school culture to have a shared goal of antiracism and understanding privilege could spur progress for the other goals. For example, the values of the school culture should always be reflected in the school mission (recommendation #1) and the professional practice goals for the district and the school improvement plan typically align with that mission as well (recommendation #3). A school culture that embraces antiracism and explores the role of privilege means that teachers and students likely understand the power of internalizing those concepts and having their actions reflect those ideas (recommendation #2). If district and strategic goals have a throughline of antiracism and understanding privilege, then teachers' professional practice goals will likely need to have a similar focus. A major factor in helping teachers develop professionally is by participating in high-quality professional development workshops or courses (recommendation #4) and having time and resources to be reflective and practice this work (recommendation #5). Likely, such professional development and reflective planning time will be structured in a way that teachers learn to utilize academic standards as leverage for racial conversations and exploring privilege. In sum, recommendations #1–5 and #7 are all influenced by #6 (school culture).

It is possible to see this approach through an opposite lens, too. School culture that focuses on openly talking about race and unpacking privilege can be developed by utilizing the other recommendations as steps in the right direction (i.e., recommendations #1–5 and #7 can help achieve #6). Either way, a school culture is all-encompassing and such a broad focus can help the other smaller action steps come to fruition. It takes all school stakeholders (parents, teachers, administrators, school committee/board members, etc.) to ask themselves what actions they are taking to contribute to a school culture with such values. It comes back full circle to Scribner et al.'s (1999) assertion that self-reflection on one's contributions toward the goal is an integral part of this process.

The Role of Race in a White School's Culture

All too often, in predominantly white schools, race is characterized in a handful of ways, which include recognizing holidays and heritage months with guest speakers and trivial events, studying a whitewashed, storybook-like version of US history, and not talking about race outside of a historical context to maintain a colorblind perspective throughout the community. However, we know, as previously discussed in this book, a colorblind perspective is toxic for many reasons. The mentality that when whiteness is pervasive, race is not present, is thus maintained. Such a viewpoint spread across an entire school's culture prevents students and faculty from acknowledging what it means to be white. When there is no one who is different in race (i.e., a person of color) to challenge the whiteness or bring in a different perspective, ignoring race altogether is what is comfortable and routine.

What would it be like for a predominantly white school to revamp its school culture? Here are some qualities that may be seen in a white school's culture that looks closely at race, equity, and the role of privilege:

1. When there is a horrific event/hate crime locally or at the national level, the school response is not simply one of remorse, but one of reflection asking, "As white people, how can we ensure we contribute toward ending white supremacy?"
2. When there are school-wide events for Black History Month, are the same figures discussed and guest speakers tokenized as representative voices of color? Or, does the school offer events that dig into uncovering silenced figures from history and modern-day? Maybe the school even rewrites some narratives that have incorrectly glorified white figures.
3. Is Black History Month or other racial and ethnic heritage months the only time race is discussed across the school community? A more pervasive approach to discuss race

that is not dependent upon special events shows that race is everywhere, every single day.
4. The physical environment communicates figures of all races thriving and embraces the immigrant makeup of the US. This is paired with updated rhetoric that matches a full desire to learn about and from people of all races and backgrounds (for example, the US is not a melting pot, but more like a tossed salad).
5. Family activities encourage parents to be involved in the process of unpacking privilege. If inner-city schools can offer English classes to immigrant parents, then why can't white suburban schools offer classes for white parents to start understanding their whiteness and role in dismantling systemic oppression?

Sparking Motivation for Cultural Shifting

Now that you conceptualize the power of school culture, how it epitomizes a supportive place to thrive in this work, and what areas it influences and vice versa, what is your role?

If you are a teacher, then think about your own professional development, academic integrations, and advocating for time to practice and reflection (recommendations #4, 5, and 7). I encourage you to consider talking to your principal, the superintendent, and even the school committee/board about what it takes to shift the school culture in the direction of antiracism and unpacking privilege. I would begin with the school and district mission statements as a starting point and then asking, "Do we see language here that communicates understanding our biases and privileges as tools to evoke societal change?" If not, then I would encourage some of the following language taken from educational institution's diversity, equity, and inclusion mission statements to be considered for your school's mission statement:

> We are committed to centering race in our pursuit of social justice and anti-oppressive practice… using a power, race, oppression and privilege (PROP) framework…We aim to foster brave spaces where students, faculty and staff can engage in critically analyzing and addressing

institutionalized racism, multi-systemic inequities, and various forms of oppression...
(Columbia School of Social Work, 2020)

It is especially critical that upon graduating...students are prepared and able to navigate, thrive and act in a diverse world...[G]raduates must be knowledgeable, empathetic and engaged about the struggles marginalized groups have faced in the past and continue to face, and they must work with confidence, passion and integrity as they help to create a more equitable, more inclusive world. [The school] both draws on and creates power and privilege; therefore, the school carries the responsibility to shape its students into graduates who will have a tangible, positive effect on their spheres of influence.
(The Brooks School, 2022, pp. 1–2)

...students will: Engage with the world: understand and think critically about local, national, and world events and societal systems; and create positive change through civic action....Students learn by engaging with diverse perspectives and apply their learning to examine the natural world and different historical, social, and political contexts
(MA Department of Elementary and Secondary Education, 2023)

The three examples above highlight the idea of privilege as a tool for action—a notion that is missed in many school mission statements/diversity, equity, and inclusion statements. What is important to highlight in these statements is that they are action-oriented for change with the mindset that societal change is in students' hands. If ideas like the ones listed above in the examples are already included in your school's mission statement, or the mission statement is successfully revised accordingly, the next question to ask is, "How do we live these values?" This could then lead to the other recommendations coming to fruition.

If you are an administrator, think about having honest conversations with faculty about what it means to foster antiracism and unpack privileges in a predominantly white setting. Make it a conversation that encourages faculty to share their perspectives on the ideas as well. What makes them motivated, hesitant, scared, uncomfortable, etc.? This is an opportunity to then share your own perspectives and the benefits faculty and students could reap from such work (recommendation #2). This is a great first step toward progress for the other recommendations with improved school culture being the end goal.

Sparking motivation in individuals is a great first step and pushback is to be expected in this process. You might be thinking something along the lines of, "I mean, I'd love to revamp our school mission statement or encourage administration to take such words more seriously with action steps, but there are so few people with my same motivation." I feel you because I was there mentally for a while, too. However, I find great hope in the "3.5% Rule." This is a concept developed by Erica Chenoweth in which she asserts that nonviolent social movements succeed when they have 3.5% of the population involved in the movement (Robson, 2019). That's it! Only 3.5% of the population can lead toward massive change. In fact, when that mere percentage was reached, change was *always* enacted. Think about the faculty and administration in your school or district. Could a mere 3.5% of those people express a passion toward antiracism and equity? As a teacher, maybe your actions within your classroom will inspire grade-level teammates, or as an administrator, your passion for antiracism may strike a chord with some students. It takes courage to face rejection and challenge. Embrace the pushback because it means you are in the right direction. Pushback means people are feeling uncomfortable, which is an unavoidable sensation in this work, further affirming you are heading the right way. Keep pushing knowing that 3.5% is a great start and can lead to change. Start small and know that it is a step toward improving a school, a district, and city/town community.

Buy-In through Facts

While you may be incredibly passionate about bringing antiracism to your teaching, you may be left dumbfounded that not everyone feels the same as you. I certainly did. I was often left baffled thinking, "how in the world is every educator and administrator not seeing that white kids need to learn about race, racism, and the role their white privilege plays in society to change the oppression we see today? How are they okay with ignoring these topics?" 3.5% can feel daunting. As much of a moral dilemma as this is for us passionate educators, sometimes the most effective method for breaking through to those who don't show the same level of motivation is to share facts and statements that I think are simply undeniable. Recruit an army of supporters for this work by showing the numbers that display why having white students understand race and privilege is important. Share statements that make them pause, even if just for a second.

Here are some ideas to share that could turn some heads and spark motivation:

- 22% of black parents discuss race often with their children, and only 6% of white parents have these conversations (Kotler et al., 2019).
    - The message here: Teachers have an opportunity to help address conversations that aren't happening at home. Who better the fill this void than teachers?
- About 35% of all parents in a survey reported that they never talk to their children about social class (Kotler et al., 2019).
    - The message here: Teachers have an opportunity to discuss the role race has with residential and income disparities. Social class discussions are rooted in race and can be opportunities for students to recognize residential racial segregation that leads to racial segregation of schools.

♦ Research shows that between the ages of 2 and 5 years, young children notice differences in gender, race, disability, and ethnicity. They become sponges for absorbing both positive views and negative biases from the significant adults in their lives. These adults are namely parents and teachers (Derman Sparks et al., 2004).

♦ The message here: The earlier that adults become aware of their own biases and see themselves as role models for promoting equity and antiracism, the greater the impact they can have on preventing biases from developing in the young children they are influencing. Kids are never too young to talk about race, like by answering their questions similar to, "Why is my skin light and that girl's skin dark?"

♦ A study by Common Sense Media (2022) found that teen and tween social media usage went up 17% between 2017 and 2021, which is much higher than four years earlier. Daily screen time increased, on average, for tweens (ages 8–12) to 5 hours and 33 minutes from 4 hours and 44 minutes and to 8 hours and 39 minutes from 7 hours and 22 minutes for teens (ages 13–18).

♦ The message here: Students are still hearing of racist events in the news and need a safe place to digest these occurrences, rather than racist sources, like on social media. Misinformation is rampant on social media and youth need adults to help them decipher what is true and what is false.

♦ Some white educators think of racism "as an issue somehow relevant only to Black people, Indigenous people, and other people of color, it's like addressing drunk driving by talking only to pedestrians" (Nurenberg, 2022).

♦ The message here: Modern horrific events based on racism (countless shootings and hate crimes) can serve as unsettling reminders that white students need to be aware that racism is not in the past and shouldn't just be contextualized as something that "came to pass" during the Civil Rights Era. Racism matters to white people because they are the ones that can stop reinforcing inequities through unconscious biases and small injustices that white people commit without even knowing it.

- Teaching through a lens of Critical Race Theory does not demoralize children and make them hate themselves (Wolfe-Rocca & Nold, 2022). It equips students to challenge white supremacy and alter the status quo. White students are more likely to feel relieved with the truth and transparency, not guilt and self-loathing.

    - The message here: When students express shame or guilt when learning the truth about race in America (both historically and today), this is an opportunity for adults to consider such feelings in a way that promotes a healthier sense of self and identity. This can be done through articulating how we don't own the actions of our ancestors, but we do have the power to influence our future actions to not perpetuate the same injustices.

The ideas and facts presented above are a meager sampling to put a sense of agency in the minds of people in your school community. Dropping them into conversations or emails, when they seem fitting based on the discussion/topic, is a great way to make clear that this work matters and cannot wait.

Parental Buy-In

While the buy-in with those who work in the schools matters greatly, parents play a monumental role. As seen in numerous states, the pushback to talking about race and utilizing approaches like Critical Race Theory has been widely criticized by conservative groups, the points listed above could be shared with the larger community as well. Sometimes it takes removing the name of "CRT" from this type of learning and cutting labels like "woke" and putting the ideas in more simplistic terms to get skeptics to see what is really happening. This is an attempt to depoliticize an education that highlights race and unpacks privilege. While countless parents who send their children to global majority schools (where there is a majority of students of color) often attend night classes to further their education or learn English, maybe it is time for privileged white parents to take some time to take night classes as well. Our society has highlighted that adults need to be adept in English and job skills, but not antiracism skills. Maybe it is time for white parents to try learning some of the lessons that address race and unpack privilege to truly see that it doesn't breed guilt in shame. Rather, these parents could experience, first-hand, that seeing the world through race shapes their actions and helps diminish their biases and perpetuation of systemic oppression. These parents, who take the time to learn and change their minds, as hard as that may be, could be the strongest proponents to help win more parental support and more support from school/district faculty and administration. This is all to say that parents can help influence the school positively and the school can influence the parents positively.

Get Some Money and Attention
While gaining support from the school community may be a "long game" part of the process of shifting school culture, keep remembering that even if not everyone is seeing the value of this work, it doesn't mean it isn't important. One thing that I learned was that it is important to get some financial support in this process. I applied for grants, fellowships, and other opportunities that would help me get training. I applied for a grant to participate in a summer professional development program through the National Endowment for the Humanities, which allowed me to study for two weeks with educators from across the US at Historic Deerfield, MA. During the summer institute titled, *African Americans in the Making of Early New England*, we learned about the silenced/forgotten voices of African Americans during the early years of our nation. There weren't any professional development opportunities for me through my district's

funding sources, so I decided to get my own funding to obtain the training I sought, and it was worth it. After that summer, my view of teaching social studies was forever changed through a decolonized lens. I forged a network of like-minded educators across the US that reminded me that even if I didn't see the same passion directly around me at work, it's there within our nation.

In addition, my acceptance to the program was featured in the local newspaper, as was some of my "different" teaching approaches. An example was when I taught the 2016 election to my fifth graders and one of our Socratic seminars was featured under the headline, "Pint-Size Pundits Dissect Debate." And you better believe race, equity, and privilege were topics of discussion in those lessons! In essence, the larger community was seeing the important work I was doing, and parents were reaching out with words of encouragement and support and the district administration appreciated the positive publicity. The lesson here: get money yourself to do the learning you need, and public awareness of your efforts may increase support.

If you are finishing this chapter feeling like a driven teacher, on a lonely island, don't despair. You have tools now to spark motivation in others, to influence those around you, and make strides within your own classroom and eventually your entire school. You see school culture as a powerful support that is possible to achieve over time. Finally, you recognize that support from others is important, but you know that you have the strength and motivation to get started independently and grow from there.

Reflective Questions

I now invite you to reflect on the ideas presented in this chapter.

1. Look at your school/district's mission statement. In what ways could it be improved to fully embrace antiracism, unpacking privileges, and promoting equity?
2. How would you describe your school culture? What is the role of race in that culture?

3. In what ways has your school/district administration communicated prioritizing racial conversations in classrooms and in what ways has it been lacking?
4. What is the parental climate like? Are parents motivated toward this work? Against it? Silent? What ideas do you have to possibly get parents on board, if they aren't already?
5. Is your school's principal approachable regarding improving the school culture with an antiracist focus? If so, what are your next steps to have a conversation about this? If not, are there other teachers who may be willing to partner in a message to the principal to evoke power in numbers? Or, is there another more approachable administrator with whom you feel like you could speak?
6. How can you inspire 3.5% of your school community to feel motivated to evoke change in your school culture? In other words, what actions could you take to share the work you're doing in your own classroom, or want to do in your own classroom if you aren't doing it already, to inspire colleagues to join the movement?
7. Which of the "Buy-In Facts" presented do you think you could share with faculty at your school to ignite some motivation to consider talking more about race in their classrooms?
8. What are some possible funding sources that could help you get the training you think could help you on your journey?
9. How might you share with the school community and greater community that work you are doing and its importance? What could that sharing do to help you increase buy-in from others at your school/district?

Dr. McGowan Weighs In

As educators, should we move away from the term multiculturalism, or should we embrace multiculturalism as an intersectional, foundational framework for our antiracist work? In answering this question, let's think about multiculturalism and how it encourages us to think about connecting to people who are different regarding the social identities discussed in Chapter 3 specifically looking at race. Multiculturalism promotes using food as a relationship connector for encouraging superficial dialogue between the races. Antiracism builds upon the important first step of establishing multicultural relationships between people by moving people toward meaningful individual and collective action toward disrupting school racism at the policy and systemic levels.

References

Boivin, J. (2020). *Exploring the role of the school principal in predominantly white middle schools: School leadership to promote multicultural understanding*. Routledge.

The Brooks School (2022). *Diversity, equity, and inclusion mission statement*. https://www.brooksschool.org/uploaded/School_Life/DEI_Mission_Final_Oct26th.pdf?1603830304035

Columbia School of Social Work (2020). *Diversity, equity, and inclusion mission statement*. https://socialwork.columbia.edu/about/dei/dei-mission-statement/

Common Sense Media (2022). *The common sense census: Media use by tweens and teens*. https://www.commonsensemedia.org/sites/default/files/research/report/8-18-census-integrated-report-final-web_0.pdf

Derman-Sparks, L., Gutierrez, M., & Bruson Day, C. (2004). *Teaching young children to resist bias: What parents can do*. National Association for the Education of Yong Children.

DiAngelo, R. J. (2018). *White fragility: Why it's so hard for white people to talk about racism*. Beacon Press.

Gay, G. (1994). *At the essence of learning: Multicultural education*. West Lafayette, IN: Kappa Delta Pi.

Kotler, J. A, Haider, T. Z., & Levine, M. H. (2019). *Identity matters: Parents' and educators' perceptions of children's social identity development*. New York: Sesame Workshop.

MA Department of Elementary and Secondary Education (2023). Educational vision. https://www.doe.mass.edu/bese/docs/fy2023/2023-05/item7.1-educational-vision.pdf

Miner, B. (1991). Taking multicultural, anti-racist education seriously. *Rethinking Schools*. https://rethinkingschools.org/articles/defining-multicultural-anti-racist-education/

Nurenberg, D. (2022, May 17). The Buffalo massacre is exactly why we need to talk about racism with white students. *Education Week*. https://www.edweek.org/leadership/opinion-the-buffalo-massacre-is-exactly-why-we-need-to-talk-about-racism-with-white-students/2022/05

Robson, D. (2019, May 13). Nonviolent protests are twice as likely to succeed as armed conflicts—and those engaging a threshold of 3.5% of the population have never failed to bring about change. *BBC*. https://www.bbc.com/future/article/20190513-it-only-takes-35-of-people-to-change-the-world

Scribner, J., Cockrell, K., Cockrell, D., & Valentine, K. (1999). Creating professional communities in schools through organizational learning: An evaluation of a school improvement process. *Educational Administration Quarterly, 35*(1), 130–160.

Wolfe-Rocca, U., & Nold, C. (2022, Aug. 2). *Opinion: Why the narrative that critical race theory 'makes white kids feel guilty is a lie*. The Hechinger Report. https://hechingerreport.org/opinion-why-the-narrative-that-critical-race-theory-makes-white-kids-feel-guilty-is-a-lie/

5

Starting Small and Keeping It Real

Resist the Urge to Run Away

As previously discussed in the early chapters of this book, a single classroom can have a significant impact on the antiracism in a school. One classroom can inspire other teachers to bring antiracism to their own classrooms and as we discussed, over time, the entire school culture can embrace such priorities. The objective of this chapter is to think about the small moments that serve as opportunities to "dabble" in equity work in our classrooms. This chapter explores how, prior to feeling ready to revamp each subject area to embrace antiracism and equity, teachers can take small incremental steps in their teaching. Some of these suggestions presented are rooted academically, while others are more responsive to students in everyday interactions.

Some of the conversations and approaches delineated in this chapter will impact white students emotionally at times. For example, learning about white supremacy and white people's acts of racism, both modern and historically, can trigger a variety of emotions. Social-emotional tactics and insights are explained in Chapter 9, but in this chapter, it is important for you to remember that white students' feelings and helping them cope with those feelings can feel uncomfortable and "sticky," but not a reason to succumb to white fragility and turn away from this work (DiAngelo, 2018). Our nation needs white teachers who resist the urge to run away from "dipping their toe in the antiracism water." Starting small is so important because if you haven't done small bits of integrating antiracism into your teaching and in the learning environment you foster, the larger curricular changes feel far too behemoth to fathom undertaking.

Personal Work Is Progressing, School Culture Goals Are Motivating, but Now What?

So, at this point, you've read four chapters that have likely motivated you and enlightened you in a variety of ways. Let's take a moment to recognize all the learning you've done so far (yes, I fully welcome you to give yourself a "pat on the back" for the work you've put in at this point).

In Chapter 1, you learned a bit about my story and what inspired this work. In Chapter 2, you saw the numbers and undeniable truth and consequences of our schools being racially segregated for students and the teaching force being predominantly white. When you got to Chapter 3, you realized before even considering being an antiracist *teacher*, you needed to work on being an antiracist *human*. Then, in Chapter 4, you saw that this isn't work that can be done in solitude forever to truly have an impact. The role of administration and the importance of equity and antiracism as a fundamental part of a school's culture are powerful goals to hold in mind as we spend the remaining chapters, including this one, focused on the actions you bring to your own classroom. Just like "Rome wasn't built in a day," a school culture that authentically embraces equity and antiracism can't develop overnight. We will start small by focusing on our own classrooms, but even within that small domain, we must start with small moments. In sum, we are starting with the smallest bits of our teaching and then growing from there by working on day-to-day student interactions and the learning environment and then thinking about the curriculum.

While some of the tactics and ideas presented in this chapter may seem doable, depending upon where you teach, there may be strict policies in place that limit your ability to talk about race out of fear of sounding "too woke." If you're teaching in a restrictive environment, consider how you may tweak or modify these approaches, along with the recommendations that appear in the subsequent chapters, based on what's plausible for you. I encourage you to remember that most decisions made regarding a school's curriculum are made at the local level. Refer to Chapter 4's ideas about school culture and how widespread prioritization of antiracism can make classroom-based instructional and curricular decisions your own.

The Elephant in the Room

Have you ever been in a situation where you don't realize something obvious until someone says it aloud? This has often happened to me when something has been normalized to the point where it doesn't feel novel or worth my attention over time. For example, my cat, Remi, is very talkative, but I've gotten so used to it that I hardly think much about it. We've had her so long that I just assume that everyone's cats are just as talkative as Remi. It takes a guest at our home pointing out how talkative she is for me to recognize that she's a vocal cat.

A similar instance happens in predominantly white learning environments. Since predominantly white schools are typically found in predominantly white residential areas, whiteness becomes the societal norm there. There's no need to talk about the whiteness because for those white folks living, learning, and working there, it doesn't impact day-to-day interactions and tasks, so why spend time talking about it? By ignoring the whiteness, the normalization of the white predominance becomes increasingly cemented and anything that could challenge the white predominance is met with increased disdain and resistance. However, if predominantly white schools rely on the normality of whiteness, they will see any sort of racial diversity as abnormal and uncomfortable. Furthermore, when whiteness is the norm, it is not discussed or recognized. This means that students lack opportunities to notice that they are white and what that means. Like how it takes a guest pointing out that my cat is talkative for me to notice that quality about her, it can take a teacher encouraging students to think about their whiteness for them to notice it.

In a piece called "Why Talk About Whiteness?", Chiariello (2016) explores white people talking about their racial identities. She writes that whiteness flies "beneath the race radar" because the reinforced ways that whiteness protects itself, and has been normalized, are foundational aspects of US systems and institutions. In short, whiteness as a norm has been, and continues to be, a defining aspect of America's character.

Chiariello (2016) quotes the creator of *The Whiteness Project*, Whitney Dow, in writing, "Until you can recognize that you are living a racialized life and you're having racialized experiences every moment of every day, you can't actually engage people of other races around the idea of justice" (Chiariello, 2016). Dow explains, "Until you get to the thing that's primary, you can't really attack racism." This notion brings a sense of urgency that if our youngest generations of white students are going to enact systemic change one day, they need to realize their whiteness early on to spark deep-rooted racial identity formation and see the role of whiteness in American society.

When everyone in a learning environment recognizes their racial identities, it opens doors for honest, hopeful conversations. As a white teacher, when it becomes normal for all members of my predominantly white classroom to identify their race openly, I can more easily model how my whiteness plays a role in my antiracism. I can connect with students on our shared racial identities and that commonality can be a powerful tool to support students on their journeys of antiracism and for students to see my actions as a role model for them. Our shared whiteness allows us to approach learning about our race through one of truth and hope. Shared racial identities can open opportunities to tap increased vulnerability, too.

As a white educator, when I model mistakes I have made (and continue to make) in my journey of becoming antiracist, it has often led to white students saying, "I've made that mistake, too!" While students may not have been comfortable admitting it organically, playing off my mistake makes their mistakes feel better because they aren't alone. It takes modeling to spur their contributions because I show it's okay to make mistakes and students respond to that relatability.

A Shared Understanding Through a Lens of Positivity

There has been a great deal of pushback in American society when it comes to addressing race in classrooms. Much of that resistance has branched from the fear that talking about race at a young age causes white students to feel bad or guilty about their whiteness (see Chapter 2). We know, however, that this is not how such conversations are structured in a safe and brave learning environment with antiracism and equity at its roots.

When openly discussing our whiteness with our students, it is first important to not shy away from the truth. As we will discuss in Chapter 7, the truth around whiteness begins through a historical viewpoint of racism in the US. As we will explore, guilt is an unavoidable emotion for white people, and part of the process, when learning about whiteness in America. It is impossible to understand true whiteness in America, both historically and modern-day, without there being a lot of ugliness explored. While guilt is inevitable for white people learning these truths, the goal of learning the truth is not to linger in a state of guilt and feeling ashamed. The truth is meant to inspire hope and proactivity. As a white person, when I learn more about the oppressive role of whiteness in society, I aspire to be a force to redefine whiteness more positively. More specifically, I strive to be an influence that redefines the word "white" as one of allyship, support, equity, and change. I desire for Black, Indigenous, People of Color (BIPOC) people to not automatically associate whiteness with oppression and prejudice. As we discussed in Chapter 4, there is power in numbers. If more white people own their whiteness with the notion that they can be one of a growing number of white people who are choosing to define what it means to be white in America, then norms will shift over time.

Understanding our whiteness comes with understanding the privileges that are embedded in that racial status. This means taking the time to work with students to understand how their race provides them with different lived experiences than students of the same age but of different races. Vignettes and examples are one of the most powerful approaches to make because it takes the abstract concept of white privilege and makes it feel more concrete.

McIntosh (1990) wrote about instances throughout everyday life that mark societal privileges based on whiteness. She gives examples like, "I can go shopping alone most of the time, pretty well assured that I will not be followed or harassed" and "I can be pretty sure that if I ask to talk to 'the person in charge,' I will be facing a person of my race" (McIntosh, 1990). McIntosh (1990) then elaborates that while we associate the term "privilege" with whiteness, a privilege is often something that has been earned. By being white, and experiencing more favorable societal conditions, those are not earned benefits. No one earns their race—we are born into it. Rather, "power" is a term that may be better fitting to describe what comes with being white in the US. In contrast, in this text, and in the antiracism literary cannon at large, "privilege" is the common term being used. However, dear reader, I encourage you to consider the term "power" as one to eventually replace the word "privilege" moving forward as our society largely begins to recognize the unearned privileges associated with whiteness.

Understanding white privilege and power, on a personal level, means taking the time to critically examine the world around us in comparison to the world surrounding people who are different from us. This can start off with having students look around their classroom and answering the prompt, "What in this room helps us learn?" and then record their observations for everyone to see. Students may contribute ideas like computers and a variety of technologies, books, art supplies, support staff, and more. Then, providing an image of the classroom from a school that is not predominantly white (but unidentifiable, of course) could be shown. The students can then see what aspects of their classroom they find helpful for learning missing from the image. This is an opportunity for students to then discuss why this is not "equitable." An important follow-up conversation would address the students' role in the future. The teacher has the great opportunity to tell students that as they grow and mature, they can help ensure all students have the type of learning environment they have. The most important aspect of this activity is to not linger on students feeling bad about what they have, and others do not. The emphasis needs to be on students' roles in the future. Depending on the age, students can discuss how lack of resources and funding for certain schools can have detrimental effects on the students at those schools into the future (i.e., lower college enrollment, unemployment, lower incomes, etc.). It is also integral to make clear that not all global majority schools struggle, but transparently showing the numbers can be a convincing factor for older students. Again, an action-oriented lens is needed so students feel activated and reflective of their roles (and maybe even their families' roles).

For our youngest students, I find Ben Sand's (2020) *A Kids Book About White Privilege* a helpful conversation starter. The approachable language and simplicity of the text can prompt curiosity and question-asking. His other texts focus on racism and systemic racism, which I also highly recommend. *Race Cars: A Children's Book About White Privilege* (Devenny, 2021) is another helpful book for opening these conversations. As you'll see in Chapter 6, literature is a great avenue for broaching these topics.

While the aforementioned activity comparing classrooms can evoke students to think about racial disparities in education, it does not acknowledge the larger systemic racism within the US. It is important that students see other examples of how the white experience in America is different than the BIPOC experience in America.

Can We Really Learn About Other Races When We're All White?

As we try to cultivate learners who recognize their whiteness and the privileges that inherently come with whiteness, we want them to learn about races other than their own, too.

A major part of being an antiracist is learning about what makes others different than us. However, it is important to recognize, within us and alongside our students, that if we are all white, we cannot fully and authentically learn about other races. We can do some learning, but without forging real-life, authentic relationships with people of other races and hearing their lived experiences, the learning that we do about other races is surface-level and sometimes risks being artificial and/or surface-level in nature.

As teachers, it is easy to fall into the rut of celebrating the same BIPOC individuals at given times of the year. For example, during Black History Month, too many teachers refer to the same people: Rosa Parks, Martin Luther King, Jr., Jackie Robinson, etc. Discussing the pre-Civil Rights Movement prejudices within a framework that claims racism in the US is part of the past, not the present, can make white teachers feel like they "checked the race box" in their curriculum and that the "deed is done." While covering important figures and events in the racial history of America is important, it is worth noting to students that it is impossible to deeply learn about and internalize something that lacks a personal quality.

As educators, we know that when we can make the content feel relatable to ourselves *and* our students, the learning is deep-rooted, engaging, and more authentic. For example, when I taught fifth grade, I brought in my passion for baking and my students' experiences baking with loved ones into how I taught fractions. Everyone in the classroom had shared experiences with baking and that improved the learning experience. As someone who has been baking for most of my life, I was able to really speak to the process through a lens of experience, and even with minimal experiences, my students were able to speak to the process through experience as well.

In contrast, if I were to try and teach a lesson about what it's like to be an astronaut, neither my students nor I can fully do that justice. We can explore astronaut life together through research, but our understanding will never be to the same extent as those who have been astronauts or who have gotten to talk or work with astronauts directly. Our learning with baking is more deeply internalized than it is with astronauts, thanks to experience and application.

A similar thought process can be applied to teaching race. As a white teacher with white students, we can research all we want, but my students and I will never be able to have the same level of understanding of what it is like to be BIPOC in America as BIPOC people themselves. The bottom line here: we can teach about race, but it's important that we and our students know that white people will never truly know what it is like to be a BIPOC in America without experiencing it themselves. Furthermore, teachers and students need to recognize that without BIPOC in our classrooms, it is more challenging for everyone to understand race in America without those relationships. It is good for students to understand the drawbacks of being racially segregated. While being at a predominantly white school may mean more instructional resources in the classroom (like they would notice in the classroom comparison example activity), the social understandings that are lacking can help motivate students to consider interracial friendships outside of school. While students saw that schools with predominantly BIPOC students may lack instructional resources, this exercise gets students to recognize that by being segregated from peers of color, their own learning is sacrificed as well. What white students may have in instructional resources and test scores, they may be lacking in shared humanity with others that are different than themselves. These understandings are all powerful tools for students to feel motivated to fight for integrated schools.

Avoiding Generalizations When Talking About "Them"

As a woman, I often get a bit annoyed when I hear someone make a generalization about women, especially if it is negative. For example, if I hear someone say something like, "women don't have as good of a sense of direction as men" I feel insulted because I feel like the great sense of direction that I have has been totally discredited.

When we teach our students about races outside of our own, it is easy to generalize, make assumptions, and talk about other races as "them." This is bound to happen at certain points when hosting conversations about a group of which you are not a part, it is easy to lump everyone of that race together. It's important that we communicate to our students that each individual has their own experiences and when we discuss BIPOC in collective terms, we must bear in mind that there will always be exceptions to the generalizations. Saying "all BIPOC," or a similarly all-inclusive phrase is never appropriate. Even the abbreviation of BIPOC is problematic, as explained in Chapter 1.

Conversation Parameters: For Students and Parents

When working with learners of all ages, we know that making content-specific and behavioral expectations clear from the start. Effective practices show that establishing clear expectations at the start of the school year is important for consistency in students following those expectations throughout the remainder of the year. As educators, we start off the year establishing classroom rules and every lesson and activity has its own expectations, as well as reminders of these broader expectations. On a yearly and a daily basis, we start early with expectations and embed reminders to help reinforce them. The same can apply to conversations about race and equity.

It is of paramount importance that we set clear guidelines for our students when talking about these topics. Depending upon the age group, the students can also help make these guidelines (like mid-upper elementary). These can be expectations that are general for any conversation related to race, bias, and social justice topics, or they can be tailored on a case-by-case basis to help structure conversations. The main objective of these conversation parameters is to achieve the following objectives for students:

1. All students feel they can share vulnerable sentiments without judgment ramifications.
2. Students can make mistakes, like using terminology related to antiracism.

3. Students openly express emotions, opinions, half-formed thoughts, and pose questions related to these topics.
4. Students can question/challenge each other kindly and respectfully.

Now that we have a sense of what we want our conversation parameters to achieve, what expectations will help get us there? There are a variety of guidelines that can help teachers host these conversations with students and being clear about what is acceptable and unacceptable is integral for these conversations to be fruitful. I find the "10 R's of Talking About Race" (Smith, 2020) to be a helpful starting point. The Rs are respect, reflect, resign, research, relearn, reset, reboot, and recognize our biases and privileges and cover the following ten points:

1. Approach the conversation with respect.
2. Put aside your preconceptions.
3. Examine your motivation.
4. Embrace the discomfort of not knowing.
5. Find out what you don't know.
6. Listen and be open to questions.
7. Internalize what you've learned.
8. Commit yourself to change.
9. Acknowledge your privilege.
10. Get comfortable with your story.

These points are incredibly powerful guidelines that could be used with a myriad of audiences; however, to put these on a piece of chart paper in your classroom and point at them as a reminder doesn't strike me as an effective approach. The meaning behind that list carries the emphasis we all ideally envision for conversations about race that take place with our students. For elementary students, however, let's unpack them in terms they can understand. Here are the guidelines, based on Smith's (2020) ideas that I think could work for middle-elementary school students and can be easily tailored for our younger learners as well, as follows:

1. **Respect those present and not present for the conversation:** This includes our peers, teachers, guests, and those whom the conversation is about.
2. **Be open to change and understand it doesn't happen overnight:** We all have ideas about others who are different from ourselves and we have to be flexible to change our thinking as we learn more.
3. **Don't run from the discomfort:** Sometimes talking about race and racism can feel strange and new. That often means that growth and learning are happening, which is our goal. Keep going!
4. **Refresh your memory as to why we talk about race:** As white people, we are not subject to the racism that BIPOC face often. The more we can learn and become aware of racism, the more we can do to stop it.
5. **Listen—it's your greatest learning tool:** Historically, white people have spoken over BIPOC. Let's practice listening so we can learn BIPOC's stories and goals and ask what they need from *us*, rather than us telling *them* what they need. It's also important that we listen to each other when we discuss social justice issues. Our opinions can be strong, but it's important that we take time to give everyone a voice, even if it's a voice saying something with which we don't agree.
6. **Practice patience:** We all come to these conversations with different experiences and knowledge and some of us may need more time to understand terms, ideas, and how to apply what we are learning. Be patient with each other and ourselves because mistakes *will* happen.
7. **Understand it's okay to not know it all and ask questions:** As white people, we don't know what it's truly like to be BIPOC. Sometimes we will have questions that will go unanswered, at least for a while. Remember—great conversations lead to more questions than answers. "I don't know, but I'd like to find out" is a great response to give!
8. **Share when something doesn't feel or sound right:** Did you hear someone in class say something that may have

sounded racist? Did you see something on the news that felt wrong? Come to your teacher first to share and they will help with next steps. It's important that we don't make peers feel bad in front of others if they make a mistake, so your teacher can help.
9. **Perfectionism has no place in this work, but self-care does:** We all carry biases and prejudices. Everyone does! It's important to recognize that we can work on them, but there'll always be biases to work on diminishing. While it can be tiring to do this work, it's important to listen to our bodies and minds and take care of ourselves. Need a break? Take it! Would writing your thoughts be a better fit today than talking? Let's do it! Don't be afraid to verbalize what you need to keep doing this work for the long haul. It's a marathon, not a sprint.

These guidelines are flexible and meant for customization. Maybe you have a predominantly white class, not an all-white class. That means some of the language should change. Maybe you have younger learners, and you need to have more basic language and focus on listening and noticing skills. The bottom line here: have guidelines that work for you and your learners. Maybe even use these guidelines when working with colleagues!

Working with Parents

As for parents, it is of the utmost importance that students are aware that these conversations are taking place at school, why they are happening, and the structures you are putting in place to ensure they are conducive, safe, brave learning experiences. There are many ways we can communicate with parents regarding these ideas and conversations. I can provide insights based on my knowledge and experience. However, depending on the state in which you teach, the political climate of the area, and other factors, you might customize this approach to fit your needs.

First, I'm a firm believer in transparency early and often. Letting parents know that you will be hosting conversations about race (ideally with principal support) and how they will be structured (like by showing the conversation guidelines you will be using) is a strong start. Emphasis on *why* these conversations matter will help justify your decision. After a year or two doing this, you may even develop a FAQ list to quell parental concerns. Citing the school mission statement, if applicable, and any other voices of support can be useful, too. Communication formats can vary. I personally found my own class blog site to be a useful tool for sharing updates, along with a paper newsletter that I sent home routinely. Gauging parental communication preferences early in the year can help ensure that parents are feeling included in the conversations about race. If they feel left out, unaware, or like this instructional decision was being kept from them, that is where trouble can brew. Strong communication can help establish and maintain positive, strong relationships with parents, making it more accessible to approach sensitive topics, like race (Poiner, 2022).

Second, I recommend asking parents about their thoughts and feelings about these conversations—it's better to know who may be resistant early before an issue arises so you may be able to take preventative measures and let the principal know. The backbone of good communication routines starts with considering communication *in* as much as you consider communication *out* (Poiner, 2022). Also, if a parent makes clear that they are hesitant about their child talking about race and social justice, it may help you understand why that student may behave in particular ways during such conversations. If a parent strongly indicates that they are against racial conversations, I highly recommend inviting them in for a conversation with you and the principal to discuss further. Often, in-person conversations can carry more weight and the fears of the parent can be quickly dispelled. Principal support, if available, at that meeting can make a difference and show a strong sense of unity and the importance of racial conversations. Buchanan-Rivera (Ferlazzo, 2022) says that school leader support is integral in response to challenging parents. If the principal isn't available, any other colleague who can come to emphasize that racial equity is the norm is a welcomed addition. In addition, Buchanan-Rivera adds that, in her experience, most school districts have mission statements that address diversity and equity. She contends, "You can leverage an institution's core values or beliefs in response to curricular critiques. One's effort to protect their child should not be rooted in the dehumanization or erasure of someone else's child" (Ferlazzo, 2022). I appreciate the shared humanity emphasis that this approach takes. I also have used the line, "It's better they talk about race and events they see on the news with me than on the school bus unsupervised and without structure because they *will* talk about it."

Third, I advise welcoming parents into the learning process. Sharing resources as you, the teacher, learn and grow helps you become relatable to parents like you're all on the same page in trying to grow and improve. In my experience, sometimes teachers can appear distant from parents and lack relatability, especially to parents who don't have college degrees. Shared learning opportunities, like attending a film screening or guest lecture, could be a great way for parents to informally connect with you and humanize you in their minds. Being on the journey *together* feels more approachable. Buy-in from parents can come when they understand that this new learning is for the betterment of their own children. As Cornelius Minor describes, be "radically pro-kid" (Newhouse, 2020). This work helps white children grow into responsible, caring, equity-prioritizing adults and also makes the nation safe for BIPOC students.

Fourth, like how parents who read with their children at home and model what is being taught in school reinforce good reading habits and promote consistent growth, the same can apply here. If parents maintain similar conversation expectations with their children and model their own learning and growth, the more effective their children's antiracist development. It's also a great opportunity to share opportunities that parents can offer their children that aren't possible during the school day. For example, Cultural Enhancement Activities are scaffolded activities that allow students to explore local and worldwide cultural histories (Ozuna, 2017). These experiences can include meeting local activists, attending social justice functions, and connecting with community members regarding issues and topics. For elementary students, Cultural Enhancement Activities can be as simple as leaving the predominantly white town routinely and meeting new people of different races and backgrounds. These can often serve as meaningful learning opportunities for parents.

Okay, so you understand that setting clear conversation expectations with students and communicating with parents are both important. You may be thinking, "wow, all this would work wonders if everyone in my school and the surrounding community were 100% in favor of racial equity—but they aren't." I hear you. Sure, many of the insights provided in this book could seem too "rosy" to work where you teach. I get that. However, we need a high bar to which to work and tailor it down from there so that one day we can all meet those high expectations. Take what works for you and aspire for the rest.

Tying Antiracism into Learning Outcomes: Social Justice Standards

As teachers, we know that it is necessary to identify the major student take-aways for each lesson. These are our learning outcomes for the lesson, which guide our assessments, activities, and overall lesson structure. The Social Justice Standards are a helpful tool for guiding teachers in this work and writing clear, measurable learning outcomes that can be integrated with academic learning outcomes (that match correlating state-specific standards/Common Core Standards) (Learning for Justice, 2022). These Social Justice Standards are divided into four domains, which include identity, diversity, justice, and action. The standards have been broken into specific outcomes and scenarios for grade ranges that include K–2, 3–5, 6–8, and 9–12. What makes these standards unique is that Learning for Justice has prioritized both prejudice reduction and collective action, whereas other programs and frameworks have previously only focused on one of those two tenets. Encapsulating both is key for our students' progress in being antiracist citizens and can help shape us as teachers as well.

Anchor Standards

Every grade level addresses identity, diversity, justice, and action, but the learning outcomes are revised to be age-appropriate. For example, the anchor standards of "students will respectfully express curiosity about the history and lived experiences of others and will exchange ideas and beliefs in an open-minded way" (Learning for Justice, 2022, p. 4) is written for grades K–2 as, "I want to know about other people and how our lives and experiences are the same and different" (p. 4). See how much more approachable that is for younger students? Also, the fact that there is a grade range for each of the learning outcomes communicates the time-consuming nature of this work. For example, for grades 3–5, for the anchor standard of Justice 12, the standards say, "I know when people are treated unfairly, and I can give examples of prejudiced words, pictures and rules" (Learning for Justice, 2022, p. 7). Based on my experience with teachers and parents alike, a common concern is that this work isn't appropriate for younger students. Thanks to the grade-tailored approach that Learning for Justice took, it is evident that this work can be effective and not be "harmful or inappropriate" early in a student's academic career.

The anchor standards are also paired with scenarios to answer the question, "what does this look like?" for each of the grade levels. It's worth noting that one example scenario is used to represent the entire anchor standard category, which is because of how multilayered a single scenario can be. For example, for the anchor category of "identity," the anti-bias scenario supplied outlines a student, Alicia, who identifies with they/them/elle pronouns and as non-binary and Latine. Alicia has already told all her teachers her preferred pronouns, but a certain teacher doesn't follow the student's preferences. Alicia decides to speak up when the teacher misgenders them by saying, "Please use my pronouns. It's important to me because they/them/elle better represents who I am" (Learning for Justice, 2022, p. 8). This single scenario covers the identity standards 1–5 by showing that the student feels comfortable regarding their many identities and the value of having overlapping identities. In addition, Alicia showed that she can talk confidently about her identity and as a Latine woman feels connected to her family history and culture.

It's also worth noting that some of these standards may seem more accessible in a predominantly white learning environment than others. That being said, some of the standards may not be plausible to achieve at an application level when all or most learners are white. Some standards may only be practically achieved at a surface-level understanding. That is the price of a predominantly white learning environment. While there may be academic learning advantages in predominantly white schools (see Chapter 1), students at these schools will unavoidably miss out on cultural competencies they would gain at global majority learning institutions.

This chapter provided some basic approaches for talking with elementary students about race in approachable, real ways that can transcend grades, states, and a variety of scenarios. I encourage you to apply these insights to the subsequent four chapters that are academic-focused. The next chapter looks specifically about addressing race in English Language Arts (ELA) (reading and writing). While the recommendations and structure of that chapter are ELA-specific, ideas like utilizing conversation guidelines and pairing academic standards with the Social Justice Standards are still highly applicable and can leverage the recommendations presented.

Reflective Questions

I now invite you to reflect on the ideas presented in this chapter.

1. Think back to the supports that helped you recognize your whiteness for the first time or even recently? What aspects of that process do you wish to bring to your students? What aspects do you wish to avoid with your students and why?
2. What is a small, everyday, example of white privilege you could share with students to help conceptualize how white privilege works? How would you structure addressing that example and encourage discussion about it?

3. How could you encourage students to understand that it is impossible to fully and truly understand the BIPOC experience in America as a white person?
4. How do we increase white students' understanding of racism if no one in the room has experienced it personally?
5. What does "authentic" racial learning look like in a white learning environment? Is it even possible?
6. Look up the Social Justice Standards on the Learning for Justice website (a quick Google Search will lead you there) and review them. How can you incorporate at least one in an upcoming lesson? How could these help you slowly revise your teaching approach?
7. Imagine this scenario: You write a newsletter to parents outlining who you will be having conversations about race and how they will be structured. You ask parents to reach out with any questions or concerns they may have regarding this. You get an email that strongly indicates that a parent is not okay with their student talking about race at all. How do you reply? What other actions might you take?
8. Imagine this scenario: You have a parent who complains that their tax dollars are spent on educating children on academics, not race. How do you respond? What other actions might you take? (Hint: think about pairing the Social Justice Standards with your state's learning standards).

Dr. McGowan Weighs In

When I see the term "woke," I think of our intersectional identities tied to social justice. In our current political climate, educators have once again been put in the middle of a divisive culture war with a zero-sum, either one solution or the other solution end goal based on whose "woke." It is time to deconstruct "wokeness" and state exactly what we as educators are focused on regarding racial equity and justice. As you have read in this chapter and the previous chapters and as you continue reading this book, the common theme is that antiracism work is complex and multifaceted.

References

Chiariello, E. (2016). Why talk about whiteness? *Learning for Justice, 2016*(53). https://www.learningforjustice.org/magazine/summer-2016/why-talk-about-whiteness

Devenny, J. (2021). Race cars: A children's book about white privilege. Frances Lincoln Children's Books.

DiAngelo, R. J. (2018). *White fragility: Why it's so hard for white people to talk about racism*. Beacon Press.

Ferlazzo, L. (2022, Oct. 24). How should educators respond to parents who criticize what's being taught? *Education Week*. https://www.edweek.org/leadership/opinion-how-should-educators-respond-to-parents-who-criticize-whats-being-taught/2022/10

Learning for Justice (2022). Social justice standards: *The learning for justice anti-bias learning framework*. https://www.learningforjustice.org/sites/default/files/2022-09/LFJ-Social-Justice-Standards-September-2022-09292022.pdf

McIntosh, P. (1990). White privilege: Unpacking the invisible knapsack. *Independent School, 49*(2), 31.

Newhouse, K. (2020, Jul. 2). 6 things anti-racist educators want grown-ups to know about teaching and raising kids. *KQED*. https://www.kqed.org/mindshift/56187/6-things-anti-racist-educators-want-grown-ups-to-know-about-teaching-and-raising-kids

Ozuna, A. (2017). Extending learning beyond the classroom with cultural enhancement activities. *Hostos Community College Digital Learning Commons*. https://commons.hostos.cuny.edu/academicaffairs/2017/11/29/extending/

Poiner, J. (2022, Aug. 23). Effective and transparent communication with parents should be a goal for schools this year. *Fordham Institute*. https://fordhaminstitute.org/ohio/commentary/effective-and-transparent-communication-parents-should-be-goal-schools-year

Sand, B. (2020). A kids book about white privilege. A Kids Book About Inc.

Smith, D. (2020, June 3). *The 10 R's of talking about race: How to have meaningful conversations*. Net impact. https://netimpact.org/blog/talking-about-race

6

ELA Approaches

Moving Beyond "Checking the Race Box"

When I talk to teacher candidates and practicing teachers about the most approachable ways to integrate antiracism into their teaching, the most common response I receive is to read books about the Civil Rights Movement or with characters that aren't white. That feels comfortable and usually convinces white teachers that by doing that, they can subtly address race without needing to take it overtly head-on. In other words, they can check "the race box" and feel good about themselves without getting into the icky-sticky parts of this work. Nothing gets too personal or controversial. Save that for their parents, right? Wrong.

Sure, reading some books is a good starting point, but by no means should it be the endpoint, like many think it is. I agree with other teachers that English Language Arts (ELA) is one of the more approachable academic areas to explore antiracism with students, due to the many opportunities to read and write to learn new things and explore perspectives, but there are many tactics that teachers can keep in mind to avoid a superficial approach. Writing can be a chance for students to *invent* and explore. They can imagine what the world *could* be, beyond what the world has been and is currently. In a nutshell, ELA can be a platform for students to consider the future in embracing shared humanity, learning about themselves and others, and considering the roles they will play in shaping an equitable world. Dear reader, the tips and recommendations presented here for reading and writing are just the beginning, so the questions at the end of the chapter are meant to encourage you to push your incorporations even past what is presented here.

Reading

Reading can be described as the gateway to learning in so many ways. After students learn to read, it unlocks endless potential to be able to *read to learn.* Reading can inspire writing and vice versa. Reading enables students to explore science, social studies, and math. To say that literacy is at the crux of all learning would be an understatement. This section will unpack how teachers can teach reading through an antiracist lens by addressing how to build an antiracist classroom library and how to craft reading lessons with antiracist values/meanings. Lessons using these texts don't need to take you off any strict curricular pacing. You can still address academic standards when using these books and examples threaded throughout show you how. This section will address books focused on four central topics: (1) kids as change-makers, (2) race and antiracism, (3) different cultures and perspectives, and (4) not about race, but with Black, Indigenous, People of Color (BIPOC) characters and by BIPOC Authors.

Literature to Inspire Kid Change-Makers
I remember a fifth-grade student of mine, Finn, who I think sums up the power of student engagement in reading. Finn was an energetic, athletic, kind-hearted boy who openly admitted that "school wasn't his thing." I was honestly tickled by the fact he would admit that to me in the first week of school. I noticed early in the fall that reading time was the most excruciating time of day for Finn. While he tolerated most other subjects, and science actually brought him some joy and engagement, reading was like pulling teeth. I made it a habit of having a one-on-one conversation with every student at the start of the school year to

learn about their academic strengths, areas of growth, interests, and aspects of school that seemed downright unappealing to them. During the meeting, Finn was uncharacteristically shy about not liking to read, which I think was out of embarrassment. He owned the fact he wasn't a fan of school but became very guarded about his feelings toward reading specifically. Our reading testing showed he was fluent and had comprehension abilities at a third-grade level and after talking to his mom, found out that reading outside of school was almost non-existent for him. When I spoke to Finn about reading, he expressed that he's always hated the books that teachers gave him. He thought they were boring and were never about things he liked. So, we started talking about what he liked, and he shared that he really enjoyed the fundraiser we were doing for the World Wildlife Fund. He said that was the best thing he's done at school for a while. I asked him what he liked about it, and he said, "it felt like I was making an impact on the world. Like, as a kid, I never get to change the world, but when we got a letter saying we saved a Narwhal, that felt awesome." This got my gears turning.

Finn wasn't engaged by the books he was given, so he read less. Less time reading corresponded to lagging scores for fluency and comprehension. How could I get Finn to read more? I was determined to find texts that connected to what motivated him. Since he shared he was passionate about how he, as a kid, could have an impact, I used that as my inspiration. I started with the young-reader version of *I Am Malala*. Learning of a young Pakistani girl's fight for female education by raising her voice, getting shot in the face, and continuing to speak out to make national and global waves was so inspiring and students could understand why she received the Nobel Peace Prize. We read this book as a class and that inspired guided discussions around equity and the power of education while also addressing standards like summarizing themes and comparing characters. See? Academic integrity is not lost with exploring social justice issues and how kids can be change-makers!

It was with this text that Finn actually asked me if we could have a longer reading block each day to get through more of the book. Finn wasn't alone. The entire class was invested in the story and the educational experiences of women in the Middle East and Southwest Asia. Such a book unlocks the topic of prejudice against a particular group and opportunities for writing reflections on how prejudices are part of US culture and actions that can be done to diminish the oppression.

The takeaway here is that the texts to which we expose our students can communicate powerful messages, especially messages that they can be change-makers, even as kids. Communicating their roles in social change, on local, regional, national, and global scales, can help students then apply these understandings when they learn about racial injustice. Learning how young people can foster determination and perseverance to see real, widespread change can be a foundational building block toward these students impacting the racial climate of our nation.

There are many different books that we can have in our classrooms, for a myriad of ages, that aren't necessarily about racial justice, but communicate kids being change-makers, which are worth considering for your classroom libraries. These include:

1. *A is for Activist* by Innosanto Nagara
2. *Grace for President* by Kelly DiPucchio
3. *Brave Girl: Clara and the Shirtwaist Makers' Strike of 1909* by Michelle Markel
4. Any of the *Mini Movers and Shakers* books by Mary Nhin
5. Any of the *Young Change Makers* books by Stacey C. Bauer
6. *How to Make a Better World: For Every Kid Who Wants to Make a Difference* by Keilly Swift
7. *If Kids Ran the World* by Leo Dillon and Diane Dillon
8. *You are Mighty: A Guide to Changing the World* by Caroline Paul
9. *What Can a Citizen Do?* By Dave Eggers
10. *Never Too Young! 50 Unstoppable Kids Who Made a Difference* by Aileen Weintraub

Having books about young change-makers is integral to our students seeing themselves as fully capable of having an impact.

These books are also an important part of developing the "change-making muscle" that is within every student. I used to tell my students that we all have a "change-making muscle," but some people exercise it more often, so it gets bigger, stronger, and can make larger, more noticeable changes. It felt it was important for students to know that the "change-making muscle" isn't something that we are born with being fully developed. It takes time, practice, and lots of mistakes for it to grow and show results. Creating a list of character traits for change-makers can help students see what qualities will help them on their journeys toward having large impacts on society one day. This list of traits, created with student input, will likely list descriptors like (but not limited to), courageous, determined, perseverant, curious, caring, and patient.

I'm an advocate for teachers to share what changes *they* want to see in the world. As white teachers, I see incredible value in sharing that we'd like to see change in America for BIPOC. Books about inspirational change-makers can get our students to see that they have what it takes to spark real change, but as teachers, it's then our job to help students see the changes that are most pressing. By pairing our conversations about change-making with discussions and explorations about race in America, we can encourage white students to see their role in helping bring racial equity to America one day.

Books Specifically Focused on Race and Equity

Reading books about race can be a fantastic way to open conversations about racism and antiracism with students. Chapter 8 will look specifically at social studies and history for exploring antiracism with students and there is bound to be a lot of overlap with how literature is used through a historical lens. As will be addressed in Chapter 8, time for social studies and history is at a premium in public education nowadays, due to increased pressure to have students perform well on standardized tests for ELA and Math. I recommend, however, trying to have modern-day conversations about racial inequity with students during ELA and save the historical perspectives, as much as possible, for the designated social studies block.

Otherwise, you could risk getting stuck in the rut of having the only books about race being through a historical lens, if ELA is the only time you can address social studies and race. If social studies is basically non-existent in your schedule, then by all means, this is your chance to address it, but don't sacrifice modern-day conversations. It's of the utmost importance that students grasp that racism is still very much a problem in the US.

Tying books about race in general and books about modern racial issues comes with some ideas for teachers to consider when crafting their lessons. First, when using these books, additional discussion time is warranted to address these topics. Second, a section of each of these lessons reviewing conversation guidelines (see Chapter 5) is integral for conducive class discussions. Third, have the mindset that the lesson could either go very short because students are quiet and possibly overwhelmed by what they are learning (especially if they lack experience talking about race or feel uncomfortable about these new ideas) or the lesson could run longer than expected and warrant a second part the subsequent day. Time can be a tricky factor to judge because racial conversations can go many unexpected ways.

When using texts about race and racial equity in a reading lesson, it is important to provide students plenty of opportunities to share their thoughts in a variety of formats to be responsive to students' preferred processing methods. With younger readers, utilize book illustrations to prompt students' engagement with the text. Since racism is based on visual appearance differences, it's important for students to identify what is different about characters who are maltreated and discuss why that's not just.

Important Terminology

Vocabulary will play an integral role in exploring books about race. Even if these terms are not present in the books themselves, these are terms that may be useful to students when contributing to discussions. Below is a list of terminology with their definitions, in middle-elementary language that you may consider for your "word wall" or anchor chart. This list is not all-inclusive, but it's a helpful starting point, as follows:

Equity: Ensuring everyone gets what they need, which may look different for different people.

Equality: Ensuring everyone gets the same thing, not necessarily what they *need*.

Justice: Social Justice: When individuals and groups ensure fairness to pursue "opportunities, freedom from oppression and the equitable distribution of resources" (Bridgewater State University, n.d.). In addition, "fairness, freedom from oppression and equitable distribution of resources are all grounded in the same basic principle: that all human beings have equal dignity and worth."

Race: The idea of dividing people into groups because of physical characteristics and giving those groups different meanings socially.
                              (Washington University St. Louis, n.d.)

Ethnicity: A culture of people in a certain region, which includes their heritage, language, faith, and traditions/customs.
                              (Washington University St. Louis, n.d.)

Racism: "The harmful belief that one's race or skin color is better than another's, and as a result, treating someone poorly based on their race. Racism can be further broken down into matters of systemic racism, structural racism, institutional racism, and more."
                              (Children's Bureau, 2021)

Non-racist: A person who does not take racist actions toward others purposefully. Antiracist: Goes beyond being non-racist. This is a person who actively works to dismantle racism and speaks out against racism when they see those actions or systems. Ally: "Anyone from a dominant or majority group that is working towards ending oppression by supporting and advocating for those in marginalized and oppressed group."
                              (University of Pittsburgh Library Systems, 2022)

Accomplice: "An accomplice uses the power and privilege they have to challenge the status quo, often risking their physical and social well-being in the process."
(University of Pittsburgh Library Systems, 2022)

Bias: Judgements about others that can often be unintentional and even unconscious. Biases can make us act different toward others due to something that is different about them than ourselves.

Prejudice: "Having an opinion or idea about a member of a group without really knowing that individual." This is different than a dislike, which "is based on information about and experiences with a specific individual."
(Anti-Defamation League, 2001)

Power: Having control over people and things. White people hold more power because of their race, which is unearned. More power means more control over others, which can make other's lives harder and make sure white lives are easier.

Privilege: An advantage that some people have over others to make their lives easier. White privilege is unearned and gives white people "a leg up" or a "head start" in society just by being white.

Segregation: Separating people into groups based on a particular quality. Racial segregation has historically been an issue in the US and continues to be an issue in public schools (i.e., black schools and white schools).

Stereotypes: "An assumption about what someone will do or how they will behave based on what social groups they belong to, such as race."
(Children's Bureau, 2021)

Global Majority: "A collective term that speaks to and encourages non-White persons as belonging to the majority in the globe, referring to people who are

racialized as Black, African, Asian, Brown, dual-heritage, indigenous to the Global South and/or racialized as 'ethnic minorities'. These groups currently represent approximately 80% of the world's population."
(Immigration Law Practitioners' Association, n.d.)

White Supremacy: Anyone who is white and thinks that the color of their skin makes them better than anyone else.

Some of the definitions provided could be expanded upon with examples with students and it is important for students to practice using the terms, not just reading about them. Visuals in the classroom are a great starting point, but to encourage implementation, it's important for teachers to model using the terms and giving plenty of examples of the terms used correctly (in books, in class discussions, etc.). For early elementary students, a shorter list with more simplistic definitions would be appropriate.

Books on Racism/Antiracism

There are such a rich variety of books about race and equity, and they can make such welcome additions to your classroom library and reading lessons. When choosing such texts, I recommend ensuring that you are having books that discuss race from different perspectives. For example, it is important to have students learn about race not just focused on the strife that people of races other than their own must face regularly in the US. Books that celebrate diversity help cast a positive light, rather than a consistent air of sadness when thinking about people who aren't white like them. Not all books about race need to be about racism. Empathy, for example, can be a central theme. With second graders, I like the book, *Race Cars: A Children's Book About White Privilege* to think about what privileges come with being white. As students listen to a read-aloud of this book, they could answer prompting questions to identify the emotional experiences of the race cars and later relate the story from white and black cars to white and black people. This lesson could address second-grade academic standards tied to identifying the main purpose of a text, which involves investigating what the author wishes to describe, explain, and answer. What follows is a list of children's books that discuss race in general terms, racism, and equity. These all have great potential to be tied to academics as well.

1. *Skin We Are In* by Sindiwe Magona and Nina G. Jablonski
2. *Amazing Grace* by Mary Hoffman
3. *Shades of People* by Shelley Rotner and Sheila M. Kelly
4. *Chocolate Me!* By Taye Diggs
5. *IntersectionAllies: We Make Room for All* by Chelsea Johnson, LaToya Council, and Carolyn Choi
6. *This Book is Anti-Racist* by Tiffany Jewell
7. *The Hate U Give* by Angie Thomas
8. *Can I Touch Your Hair?: Poems of Race, Mistakes, and Friendship* by Charles Waters and Irene Latham
9. *Why?: A Conversation About Race* by Taye Diggs
10. *How to be a Young Antiracist* by Ibram X. Kendi and Nic Stone

The books above make great additions to your classroom libraries and can serve as texts to use in reading lessons. These books pair particularly well with books that look at race and racism through a historical lens during social studies time, which will be unpacked in Chapter 8.

Books That Share Different Cultures and Perspectives

Literature can be a powerful doorway to learning about other cultures, races, and ways of life. I encourage you to consider stocking your classroom libraries that expose white students to books that explicitly explore other races, cultures, religions, and more. Like how books about race all don't need to be about racism, books about different cultures and races can be exploratory and celebratory, rather than cast in a shadow of telling tales of oppression. If students just hear about how BIPOC face prejudice and inequity, then they miss opportunities to learn about how people of different races can be such valuable people in our lives. As white people, we can learn so much from people who are not white. Centering whiteness is a common criticism of this approach, but when whiteness is all around in the learning environment, it's necessary to use that commonality as a basis for the conversation. Positive cultural and racial explorations books include the following:

1. *Festival of Colors* by Kabir Sehgal
2. *The Proudest Blue: The Story of Hijab and Family* by Ibtihaj Muhammad
3. *Fry Bread: A Native American Family Story* by Kevin Noble Maillard
4. *Stolen Words* by Melanie Florence
5. *Eyes That Kiss in the Corners* by Joanna Ho
6. *I am Enough* by Grace Byers
7. *Danbe Leads the School Parade* by Anna Kim
8. *Sulwe* by Lupita Nyong'o
9. *Lubna and Pebble* by Wendy Meddour

Stocking your room and lessons with a diverse array of books is evidently very important. You may have heard of Rudine Sims-Bishop's work regarding books serving as mirrors, windows, and sliding glass doors (Lesley University, n.d.). She describes books as sometimes windows, which provide us with a myriad of views of the world and these worlds can be real, imagined, familiar and/or strange. She adds that windows can be sliding glass doors since readers "have only to walk through in imagination to become part of whatever world has been created and recreated by the author" (Lesley University, n.d.). A book can be a mirror if it reflects aspects of us, and when the conditions are just right, she contends, a window can serve as a mirror at the same time. I enjoy this analogy because it gets us to critically examine the texts of which our students are exposed.

Books Not about Race, But with BIPOC Characters and by BIPOC Authors

The landscape of children's literature has been shifting over the recent years but still has a long way to go. Representation matters in our classroom libraries. Even a book as simple as a little black boy enjoying fresh snowfall carries meaning in our classrooms (see Ezra Keats' *The Snowy Day*). It disrupts the white norms of children's literature. Children's literature has a long history of being predominantly centered on white main characters. Nancy Larrick wrote, "The All-White World of Children's Books" in 1965, and this issue is still prevalent today (Northern Illinois University Newsroom, 2015). As Melanie Koss states, "People want to read about themselves but if you never see yourself in a book, what does that tell you about how you are valued? You're not" (Northern Illinois University Newsroom, 2015). Koss' look at how even when children's literature has African American characters, the Civil Rights movement, often, is the focus. She contends that it is necessary for teachers to have books that have similar plots to those with white characters, but the main characters just happen to be Black. What's unsettling is that publishers have lacked motivation to come out with books that have diverse characters because they don't see value for profits. So, it all comes down to money. However, the tides have been changing, especially in the wake of the racial justice uprising of the summer of 2020 in the US. In a world where the global majority is not white, isn't it about time that children's books reflect that reality?

Author representation matters, too, especially if the book centers around BIPOC characters. As discussed previously in this book, each of our races comes with biases and our own set of lived experiences that are different from those of another race. If I, as a white woman, were to write a children's book about a black boy in America, there may be some value to the story, and it would contribute to the cannon on literature that goes against the white predominance, but it would lack authenticity in perspective. My white woman biases would likely seep through in some ways. I suggest being aware of the authorship of the books you choose when diversifying your classroom texts.

As you revamp your classroom library with books about race, equity, and change-makers, I encourage you to also decenter whiteness as a norm by having more books about BIPOC characters. Even if such books don't directly discuss the character's race or even their cultural background necessarily, these books are important. Interestingly, when trying to make this list, it was not easy to find books that simply have a character that is not white. The character's race and culture, more often than not, play a role in the book's plot and character development. This is because social norms shift for different races. So, in the list below, the character's race and cultural background either don't play a role or play a minor role in the book. What this communicates to students is how prevalent race and cultural differences are in our society, even in subtle ways. It's impossible to think that a white child and a black child, placed in the same situation, would have the same experience, but some books make that assumption. For example, *Ada Twist Scientist* is on the list below and it does a great job depicting a young Black girl pursuing her interest in science. That's great! However, it doesn't address the obstacles and barriers that lie ahead of her in life following this career path that a white girl wouldn't face. The book is great because it shakes up the norm of white kids dreaming of being scientists, but we must be aware of how these books lack some of the realities that are inherently part of our society due to systemic oppression. That could even be a discussion point for older students. I encourage you to consider these titles for your classroom and lessons:

1. *Last Stop on Market Street* by Matt de la Peña
2. *Whistle for Willie* by Ezra Jack Keats
3. *Mango, Abuela, and Me* by Meg Medina
4. *Stand Up, Yumi Chung!* by Jessica Kim
5. *The Day You Begin* by Jacqueline Woodson
6. *Twenty Yawns* by Jane Smiley
7. *Ada Twist Scientist* by *Andrew Beaty*
8. *Esperanza Rising* by Pam Munoz Ryan
9. *From the Desk of Zoey Washington* by Janae Marks
10. *The Crossover* by Kwame Alexander (now a series)

Writing

Writing can be such a powerful tool for students to explore themselves. As an adult, I find writing of all kinds to be almost therapeutic. Writing helps me make sense of the world, challenge norms, explore more about myself, and synthesize new understandings. I guess if I didn't like writing, you wouldn't be reading this book, right? Writing is part of how I learn and grow as an educator and as a person.

When I first learned how to teach writing, I used Lucy Calkins' "Writing Workshop" and knew nothing other than that. However, since then, I have come to realize this method's flaws. Other than the curriculum making vast assumptions of young writers' abilities and not being responsive to struggling learners, the lack of opportunities to integrate other subjects into writing was a lost opportunity (Wexler, 2021). Calkins claims that her focus on writing as a method doesn't lend itself to using writing to learn about social studies, for instance. With social studies being such a miniscule amount of time each week, if at all, in most US public school classrooms nowadays, reading and writing blocks can often be the only time that students get to learn about the nation's past. Chapter 8 will go in greater depth about how history can be explored through reading and writing, but these topics should be kept in mind when considering the other recommendations provided in this chapter. This critical view of Lucy Calkin's very popular writing curriculum is just one example of how teachers can view their school/district's writing curriculum through a critical lens. I'm advocating for teachers to use mandates as guidelines and then work from there. So, if you need to use Lucy Calkins' writing workshop, can exemplar texts and prompts be tweaked to cover racial topics and/or involve BIPOC representation? Could writing prompts be used to explore racial identities and biases? These are considerations worth making if such curricular mandates are in place.

This section will address how writing can be an opportunity for students to explore racism and antiracism, learn about their own racial identities and biases, and learn about their roles in promoting social change by researching, as well as using their imaginations.

Writing to Learn About Racism and Antiracism Through Writing

Writing block can be a great opportunity to write about racism and antiracism as students formulate their understandings.

Have you ever heard the idea that you know something well if you are able to teach it to others? I am a firm believer that if you can clearly explain a concept in your own words, in writing, that shows a deepened level of compression of the idea.

Writing about race can help students learn about race. Professor Steve Graham and colleagues at Arizona State University synthesized data from 56 students and came across the meaningful common thread that writing enhances the learning process in all grade levels (Terada, 2021). While it is common for teachers to have students write about a concept or topic to see if they understand it, the actual process of writing can be key. They contend that writing helps students recall information, build connections between ideas, and synthesize content in new ways. Writing isn't just a means to assess, rather, it is a means to promote learning even further. Research has also shown that writing about a topic can enhance a students' memory if they are asked to write about it, too (Terada, 2021). An additional benefit about writing about a topic is that it can deepen understanding when a writing prompt is metacognitive in nature. What does this mean? Basically, if the prompt gets students to think about the topic with their own and/or others' perspectives in mind, the content feels more relatable. In a nutshell, writing helps aid in deeper learning, and with the complex nature of antiracism, writing can be a useful tool to enhance internalization of ideas.

"All About" writing or expository writing asks students to describe or explain something. This type of writing can address concepts like racism and equity. These assignments can be research-based, through a historical lens (see Chapter 8), or have a modern-day focus to emphasize that racism is very much alive in the US. Current event reading can be a prime opportunity for students to develop critical media literacy skills and questioning if news sources are biased, especially when it comes to politics (Spinner, 2022). In this writing, students could explain and provide details about a topic, person, movement, or event. Even "how-to book-writing" has a place here, where students might outline how to be antiracist or how to learn about their biases. Learning and writing about topics in-depth and seeing viewpoints surrounding those topics allow students to craft their own opinions. An awareness of their own opinions around a topic can help students understand if their objectivity comes out in their writing and can lead to a sense of what it means to write for your audience (Garcia & O'Donnell-Allen, 2015).

Learning About Ourselves Through Writing

Writing about race and racism in a general sense, as described above, can tell us as writers if we know little about something and need to learn more. It can be a humbling experience and there is just as much value in discovering you don't know something, as there is if you do know something. Writing with the intentionality of learning about ourselves can be even more prevalent in a variety of specific writing formats. These include journals, memoirs, public narratives, and personal reflections. And like with most writing types, there is overlap among these options, and this section is not meant to be exhaustive regarding all the ways writing can spur self-learning, rather, this subsection provides some approachable options to try.

Journaling can be a great platform for exploring ideas about race and racial scenarios. Journaling can help children deal with a vast array of emotions, can improve children's writing skills, and can enhance a child's communication skills because it can feel easier than speaking (Rodriguez, 2017). This method of writing can feel low-stakes and is typically ungraded. A dialogue journal is a great method for having a back-and-forth with students about their ideas, too. Journals can also be left unread, so students see it as a safe space to try things out. "Wonder journals" and travel journals supply consistent foci for students' journaling practices (Terada, 2021). These journaling approaches can be tied to race. For example, for "wonder journals," students can write what they wonder about regarding race and racism, and for travel journals, students can write about their experiences noticing the role race places and the racial diversity of different places and the implications tied with that socially. Interestingly, as I investigate journaling as part of writing curricula, I have found it to be a lesser-common method of writing. Materials about the power of journaling in learning about race have been in the form of parents encouraging their children to journal and how teachers can benefit from routine journal writing. I recommend considering all these domains for journaling (students at home and at school, teachers personally and professionally) as beneficial on our journeys of antiracism. Some reflective prompts, for students and adults, could range from, "In what ways have I been treated differently by others, or by society, because of my race?" and "Am I uncomfortable talking about racism with others? Why might that be?" (Milam, 2020). Sometimes a lack of structure, like what journaling can provide, is what we all need when digesting information about what it means to be an antiracist.

Memoir writing can be a prime format of writing to encourage students to learn about themselves. I recommend this process, like most writing processes, begins with a graphic organizer. "Identity wheels" provide different identity layers and students can enter in where they fall in each category. Examples of the categories include gender affiliation, socio-economic status, race and ethnicity, religion/spirituality, and more. Each of these areas can then be tied to privilege/power and oppression. For a predominantly white class, this can be a gateway for discussing white privilege. For example, as students practice memoir writing, they may have a section that explores their privileges. Another visual aid for students in learning more about themselves is "Me Mapping." This is a great option in which, "Learners engage in activities focusing on important milestones in their lives, their families and friends, experiences at home and at school, languages and cultures, and their hopes and aspirations for their future" (Ontario Institute for Studies in Education [OISE], n.d.). Identity work, like described in the "identity wheel," can be a part of this process because students can think about the role of what societal privileges, areas of power, and societal oppressions that played roles in their journeys. However, both of these approaches can serve as their own powerful stand-alone activities. Memoir writing focuses on one problem and one solution, grounded in the author's experiences (Wheeler, 2020). An example prompting question that could help students focus on race or privilege would be, "What's your first memory about race?" They then can answer sub-prompts like, "Why is that memory so vivid? What did you learn from that experience? How did you feel before, during, and after? Did it affect any relationships you have?" There are a myriad of prompts online that focus on race, biases, and other related topics, so I recommend investigating what prompts are a good fit for your students, and even *you*!

Public narratives are a branch of memoir and can be a powerful form of writing for students to explore as readers and to try themselves as writers. *I Am Malala* is an example of one (Spinner, 2022). It's someone telling their story to serve as a call to action for widespread change. Emotion plays an important role in inspiring social change, so a topic that students feel connected to is paramount. Students who write public narratives could share about the impact that learning about their biases has made them a more positive contributor to society and how others should do the same to help end racism in the US.

As simple as they are, we cannot forget the value of personal reflection writing. These can overlap with journal writing and can be kept personal or made to share. While journals are more routine, I think of self-reflections as stand-alone pieces. Self-reflection is cited again and again in antiracist literature as integral for understanding the biases we hold and uncovering those that were previously unconscious (Williams, 2010). It's important to remember that biases are learned. We are not born with them, which means the sooner that teachers and parents can work to avoid their own biases impacting their children/students, the better chance those young minds won't carry those same biases. However, depending upon the grade you teach, you may have noticed you have students who have more/deeper biases. I know I did when teaching fifth grade at a predominantly white school. By the time students have reached fifth grade, if no meaningful effort was put in by both parents and teachers early on, then those students will undoubtedly have more biases than if that effort were instituted earlier in their lives to lessen their exposure to adults' biases. Prompts that encourage students to consider why they didn't like a person, place, or thing can be a great starting point for uncovering biases, and this type of reflection can be inspired by a book you read in class (Williams, 2010). Don't forget to model your own self-reflective work and how you've unpacked your own biases, as well as what you've been doing to address them.

Writing as Change-Makers

In the reading section, we looked at the value of children's literature that highlights children impacting the world. These texts can be used for informational and creative writing prompts. This subsection looks specifically at creative writing and informational writing as tools for students to explore their roles in igniting racial equity. In fact, writing can be considered one of the most impactful forms of activism and students should know the value of the written words via examples of letters to legislators, informational pamphlets, songwriting, poetry, and more (Spinner, 2022).

Creative writing is a favorite among many students and can serve as a tool for students to dabble in the idea that they can change the world. Writing creatively can feel fun, and the added wiggle room of getting to take writing in your own direction is freeing. Creative writing can serve as a great opportunity for students to consider the world they yearn to see, after being exposed to the injustices that exist in it. Assignments like, "If I were President" put students in the driver's seat as to what changes they think are needed to establish racial equity. Activities such as this can get students to see themselves as change-makers, as inspired by great literature like described earlier in this chapter. Another creative writing prompt could be, "What a world without racism would look like." Even if students aren't explicitly stating their roles, it encourages them to think about a more equitable society and the value of that, which could be a motivating activity. Such a prompt could be a precursor to a research-based assignment, as described next.

Nonfiction writing is an important genre of writing for students because it has students consider what they know about a topic and pushes them to research more to go beyond what they know (Cohen, 2006). It's been shown that children write more fiction than nonfiction, but that it is likely due to peer influence (i.e., what the popular opinion is among students). Maybe non-fiction writing needs to level up its curb appeal by including our students more in the topics. Let's think about more practical impacts that students can have on the world, while they are still kids. This is far from the stock and standard report on a person or place. Students can explore what they can do to support racial equity. The class can research a variety of approaches and then each student can write about how they plan to follow through on that action step. One action step could be supporting BIPOC businesses over large corporate vendors. So, at the student level, maybe they are going to talk with their families about the products they buy and be more mindful about those choices. Another action step a student may explore is taking the time to address our biases by increasing our familiarity with those who are different from ourselves. For example, if a student realizes that they didn't know that there are differences between Japanese, Korean, and Chinese cultures, they can make a plan as to how they will learn more about each. It's important to use writing as a means for students to think about what they can do as kids to bring racial equity to the country, even as seemingly small acts. This is students' chance to "invent" the world they wish to see.

Another idea for nonfiction writing is to have students write about what they want to be "when they grow up" and how that occupation can play a role in dismantling racism in the US. For example, being a Broadway star, at first glance, may not seem to have the same potential to have an antiracist impact as other occupations. However, someone on Broadway could choose to only audition for productions that don't restrict roles based on race, since Broadway's history has been predominantly white. Being a Broadway star, or any position that leads to fame, comes with a public platform to speak truth to power, too. Maybe at first glance a medical doctor doesn't have a role in ending racism, but what about the rampant racism found in the treatment, or lack thereof, of Black people in the US? Every doctor has the choice to not contribute to those statistics and encourage others to do the same. Let's encourage our students to see themselves as antiracists today and as the antiracists of the future.

Empathy and equity "operate hand in hand" and should be emphasized as much as any of the standard subject areas (El Mallah & Pfister, 2022). Empathy, as a social-emotional skill, will be explored in greater depth in Chapter 9. However, I'd like to highlight how writing can be a prime opportunity for students to foster empathy toward others. Creative writing, informational writing, and self-reflective writing can come together in the form of perspective-taking exercises/projects that can spur empathy. These types of assignments encourage students to see life through someone else's shoes. Literature about people who are similar, yet different from us, books about people from a different place, and any piece of writing that challenges our assumptions can serve as great inspirations for cultivating empathy in our students (Gil, 2017). Sometimes this is in the form of having students continuing a story further like, "what would happen if there was another chapter to this book?" Such a prompt involves creativity, a grasp of the topic and characters' personalities (through research if a true story), and the ability to self-reflect if their writing is truly embodying the character's perspective. Other prompts can encourage students to put themselves in a character's place and explore how they would handle certain situations. Perspective-taking writing is a valuable opportunity to gain empathy toward others and also become aware of biases and misunderstandings that they may have previously held.

As you make your way through Chapters 7–10, reading and writing will appear numerous times, which serves as a reminder that the writing prompts and structures we provide, the books we make accessible to our students, and the prioritization of humanity we bring to our teaching, are important throughout the entire academic day and year.

Reflective Questions

I now invite you to reflect on the ideas presented in this chapter.

1. How can you encourage your students to practice using the terminology defined in this chapter? What strategies or tools may help?
2. Take a look at your classroom library and critically examine the types of books you have. How could you

improve upon the selection you offer students for reading assignments/pleasure reading?
3. Examine the texts that you use for your ELA lessons. How might you replace some of these books to increase BIPOC representation and use texts that can lead to meaningful racial conversations and explorations of social justice issues?
4. In an era where banning books seems to be a consistent headline, it's important to know if there are policies and procedures in place that keep community members from banning books in your school just because of their own prejudices. In short, it's important that it's not too easy and solid, clear justification is needed with evidence that the person petitioning the book has actually *read* the book. What's your school/district's policies around banning books? What processes must a parent follow if they don't want a book available to students? Could the policies be improved to ensure racially diverse, and social justice-oriented texts are available to students of all ages?
5. Are you offering students a mixture of opportunities to write about race and racism? Out of the various formats explained in this chapter, which is missing or offered least? Why is that the case and how might you refine your approach to writing based on what you learned?
6. This chapter mentions the value of teachers sharing with their students what social justice issues matter to them? In 3–5 sentences, in student-friendly language, can you summarize why antiracism matters to you? Can you summarize why antiracism should matter to your students?

Dr. McGowan Weighs In

As an African American man, I am very focused on historical and contemporary antiracist work relative to the African American community. However, over the years, I have learned that in addition to my African American focus, I also have to work in solidarity with other races inclusive of biracial and multiracial people and children as we work toward racial equity and justice. Often biracial and multiracial children may feel that they have to choose one racial identity over the other. As educators, we have to ensure that biracial and multiracial children can embrace all of their racial identities. As outlined in this chapter, ELA provides many opportunities for educators to teach children how to explore the dynamic prism of racial identities focused on how we are the same and how we are different.

References

Anti-Defamation League (2001). What to tell your child about prejudice and discrimination. https://www.houstonisd.org/cms/lib2/TX01001591/Centricity/Domain/13777/Prejudice.pdf

Bridgewater State University (n.d.). *Martin Richard Institute: A catalyst for social justice.* https://www.bridgew.edu/center/martin-richard-institute-social-justice#:~:text=A%20Catalyst%20for%20Social%20Justice&text=Fairness%2C%20freedom%20from%20oppression%20and,of%20Martin%20Richard%20in%202015.

Children's Bureau (2021, Jan. 11). *Racism definition for kids and teaching about stereotypes.* https://www.all4kids.org/news/blog/racism-definition-for-kids-stereotypes/

Cohen, G. (2006, Aug. 3). The benefits for children of writing nonfiction. *BU Today.* https://www.bu.edu/articles/2006/the-benefits-for-children-of-writing-nonfiction/

El Mallah, S. & Pfister, T. (2022, Feb. 1). Empathy as a tool for equity. *The Association for Supervision and Curriculum Development.* https://www.ascd.org/el/articles/empathy-as-a-tool-for-equity

Garcia, A., & O'Donnell-Allen, C. (2015). *Pose, wobble, flow: A culturally proactive approach to literacy instruction.* Teachers College Press.

Gil, C. (2017, Feb. 17). Teach empathy with literature. *Edutopia.* https://www.edutopia.org/discussion/teach-empathy-literature

Immigration Law Practitioners' Association (n.d.). *People of the Global Majority.* https://ilpa.org.uk/people-of-the-global-majority/

Lesley University (n.d.). *How to use children's literature to support anti-racist education.* https://lesley.edu/article/how-to-use-childrens-literature-to-support-anti-racist-education

Milam, B. (2020, June 13). *10 journaling prompts about racism.* https://www.briemilam.com/blog/2020/6/13/10-journaling-prompts-about-racism

Northern Illinois University Newsroom (2015, June 2). *White, white and read all over.* https://newsroom.niu.edu/white-white-and-read-all-over/

Ontario Institute for Studies in Education [OISE] (n.d.). *About me mapping.* https://sites.google.com/view/memapping/me-mapping/about-me-mapping?authuser=0

Rodriguez, J. (2017, July 20). How journaling benefits your child. *Scholastic.* https://www.scholastic.com/parents/books-and-reading/raise-a-reader-blog/how-journaling-benefits-your-child.html#:~:text=Journal%20writing%20can%20help%20your,skills%2C%20and%20communicate%20their%20ideas.&text=Journaling%20encourages%20your%20child%20to,write%20daily%20(or%20more!)

Spinner, E. (2022) *Encouraging activism in secondary English: Reading and writing for social justice.* (Publication No. 3833) [Doctoral dissertation, Western Michigan University]. https://scholarworks.wmich.edu/dissertations/3833

Terada, Y. (2021, Jan. 7). Why students should write in all subjects. *Edutopia.* https://www.edutopia.org/article/why-students-should-write-all-subjects/

University of Pittsburgh Library Systems (2022, Dec. 20). *Anti-black racism: History ideology, and resistance—Oakland campus.* https://pitt.libguides.com/antiracism/ally

Washington University St. Louis (n.d.). *Race and ethnicity self-study guide.* https://students.wustl.edu/race-ethnicity-self-study-guide/

Wexler, N. (2021, Nov. 21). Problems with Lucy Calkins' Curriculum go beyond reading—to writing. *Forbes.* https://www.forbes.com/sites/nataliewexler/2021/11/21/problems-with-lucy-calkins-curriculum-go-beyond-reading-to-writing/?sh=1e6d032850c9

Wheeler, C. (2020, Dec. 10). *Exploring memoir writing with children.* Spokane County Library District. https://www.scld.org/exploring-memoir-writing-with-children/#:~:text=Memoir%20is%20simply%20writing%20about,place%2C%20object%2C%20or%20event.

Williams, D. (2010). *Beyond the golden rule: A parent's guide to preventing and responding to prejudice.* https://www.learningforjustice.org/sites/default/files/2017-07/Beyond_the_Golden_Rule_6.pdf

7

Math and Science Approaches

When you think of integrating antiracism in your teaching, I doubt math and science are the discipline subjects you first think of, am I right? For me, I think of social studies and English Language Arts (ELA) as the ones that seem to go far more hand-in-hand with antiracism. However, don't be fooled. There are plenty of opportunities for implicitly and explicitly discussing race and racism when teaching math and science. In this chapter, we will unpack ways to disrupt the white, male archetype of mathematicians and scientists, thread a variety of multicultural norms into class activities, and provide students with projects that ask them to explore racism through issues in science and substantiating findings numerically. If teaching math intimidates you to start with, stick with me. You might find the strategies presented in this chapter as a means to make your math instruction feel more meaningful and less rote.

Shifting Who Does STEM Through Uplifting Others

I teach the elementary math methods course to our undergraduate teacher candidates and every semester I ask my students to share with me what first comes to mind when I ask them to close their eyes and imagine a mathematician. The common description is something like this: old, white man (usually with glasses but sometimes looking like Albert Einstein). My colleague does a similar exercise in science methods and white males again reign supreme as the archetype. We know that it is important for Black, Indigenous, People of Color (BIPOC) students to see figures who share common traits, like gender affiliation, and race, to help them see themselves in those roles. But what about white students? Why should they see figures that challenge the white male norms of math and science? The main reason: white students, who are inspired by BIPOC scientists/mathematicians, can play roles in un-whitewashing discipline norms.

Interestingly, when researching for this chapter, I have found plenty of articles and resources that discuss antiracism in science and math but with a focus on how teachers can make these disciplines accessible and appealing to BIPOC students to help diversify those fields in the future. There is not nearly as much information available about using science and math as vehicles for exploring racism and how to be an antiracist. As we redefine who are mathematicians and who are scientists with our students, we can talk to students about how they can help in the mission of redefining who are mathematicians and scientists.

I contend that every white person who pursues math and science has a prime opportunity to support others. Our students can lift themselves up by lifting others. I use myself as an example. The teaching profession is predominantly white and female, as is teacher preparation in higher education. I fully take ownership that my identity as a white woman has dictated much of my career path and I have benefited greatly from being a white woman in my career. No, it's not particularly pleasant to admit, but it's true. After owning this fact I'm able to do what matters: put in the hard, truth-seeking reflective work we talked about in earlier chapters. However, with this platform, I want to support others and change these norms. With that motivation, I have worked to support BIPOC friends and colleagues to get their doctorates, get published, and find jobs within education. I do committee work focused on institutional policies and development and write prices dedicated to diversifying the teacher workforce. I fully recognize that I'm pushing against a system that has benefited me greatly but at the cost of limiting opportunities for others. Recognizing it was only the beginning. Doing something about it is where the *real work* begins.

I use this example because I think it connects to the fields of math and science. While these are still very male fields, the women and non-binary people who do break through are typically white. For example, of the women working in STEM positions in the federal sector, the majority (66%) were white and African American/black women were the second-highest represented race, at a mere 14.58% (US Office of Federal Operations, 2019). Teachers can pose a call-to-action to students that regardless of gender affiliation, they can do their part to support BIPOC in breaking through as well. It's important to know that even as white people, they can still pursue careers in areas that are currently predominantly white, but emphasizing that as a white person, they hold a serious responsibility to support people of all backgrounds in succeeding in that field and not accept the whitewashed status quo. The racial barriers have been even more barricading than those of gender. Showing these sobering statistics can serve as powerful motivators for students to be involved in raising others.

Racism, too often, poses barriers that keep brilliant minds from being able to reach their full potential and have the impacts they could. When students see examples of incredible BIPOC mathematicians and scientists, they are exceptions to the norm. Teachers can tell students that if racism kept these minds from doing what they do best, then many innovations and accomplishments would have been lost. Think of all the times racism "won?" Our society probably has missed out on some insanely amazing discoveries, inventions, and feats just because society didn't want the minds of BIPOC in the fields of math and science. Why would we not want more brilliant minds improving human's lives and well-being? Racism limiting who can and can't be scientists and mathematicians is putting limitations on innovation and progress. Plain and simple. When we need mathematicians and scientists to make discoveries that improve our lives, why would we limit who can do this work? For instance, there could be a black girl who has the ingenuity to create a cure for cancer, but just because she's black, society is going to make it even harder for her to get her degrees and get a job doing that research. Society is hurting itself by limiting who can pursue what pathways. Bringing global voices to these fields is a step toward decolonizing them (American Society for Microbiology [ASM], 2023). In sum, math and science are not objective spaces, so it is essential for educators and students to consider what and who have been excluded, and at what costs. White students have the potential to amplify BIPOC voices in math and science for the betterment of humanity.

Culturally Responsive Pedagogies: Decentering Whiteness as a Step Toward Fighting Systemic Racism

Have you heard of "culturally responsive" teaching practices? It's become a very popular phrase in education and typically within the domain of racially diverse learning environments. Gay (2018) states that culturally responsive teaching involves utilizing cultural knowledge, experience, and performative evaluations more approachable and relevant to a greater diversity of students. The result is that the learning community feels welcoming and nurturing for all and free of stereotypes, prejudices, racism, and other forms of oppression. In short, teachers learn about their students and see how they can have their teaching align with students' identities. When curricula match the white-centered societal norms, they are not responsive to BIPOC lives. So, if teaching in a culturally responsive way means my instruction should match my students' backgrounds, if I have an all-white class, that means the work has already been done for me, right? Nope.

Culturally responsive teaching for predominantly or all-white classes, I propose, has a tweaked definition. I contend that culturally responsive teaching for white students isn't about aligning with students' norms, but rather, disrupting their perceptions of what is normal. In other words, we are responding to their white culture, which routinely ignores BIPOC voices, experiences, and cultures. When teaching white students, it's about instilling a little bit of discomfort in the familiar to promote questions and exploration of cultures different than their own. Our nation has a long history of establishing white norms as the "gold standard" and expecting BIPOC to assimilate whenever possible if they want to function in society. It is now time to ask white folks to assimilate to the new normal that doesn't revolve around white supremacy. The summer of 2020 racial reckoning was a wake-up call for many people to think critically about what they say, do, and with whom they surround themselves. The more that curricula can decenter white, cisgender, heterosexual, Christian norms, the more our students will see and appreciate how diverse of a nation we have. They should understand that the global majority is not white, and eventually, the US population will not be as white. Based on US Census data, "For the first time, nonwhites and Hispanics were a majority of people under age 16 in 2019, an expected demographic shift that will grow over the coming decades" (Associated Press, 2020). If our future students are going to keep up in a diversifying nation with a heightened awareness of systemic racism, they need to learn in contexts that do not center whiteness.

Disrupting white norms can feel uncomfortable, likely more so with age, due to being more used to white norms and possibly being aware of benefitting from systemic racism by being white. Removing whiteness as the norm can be a powerful step toward dismantling systemic racism. Let's briefly discuss systemic racism so it is clear why decentering white norms matters so much.

Being aware of systemic racism is very important for white students to understand to help others become aware and proactive. White students who recognize systemic racism can help shift the large portion of the white population still not believing systemic racism exists. Even in 2022, 29% of white Americans said they don't believe systemic racism exists in the US and 18% were unsure (Johnson, 2022). That's 47% of white Americans not able to say that systemic racism clearly exists in the US, even after seeing the horrendously disproportionate effects of the COVID-19 pandemic on BIPOC communities, the highly publicized, brutal deaths of numerous black Americans by police officers, and the clearly unequal financial and residential statuses for BIPOC on a national scale, there are still so many white Americans not willing to admit that systemic racism exists? Ignorance is bliss, perhaps? How can change happen if this remains? Change is still possible, but it sure would help to get more of these white folks onboard to reality. These amounts were much higher than those surveyed and identifying as black or African American, Asian or Pacific Islander, and Hispanic. Makes sense though, right? BIPOC people, who are more often oppressed by systemic racism, are the ones who are more likely to state it exists. So, let's use math and science as opportunities to decenter whiteness as a step toward fighting systemic racism.

Nabb et al. (2020) recommend rewriting problems transparently, so students are aware that you made the changes. It is powerful to show students that having whiteness at the center of everything is a part of our nation's past and still makes its way into our classrooms and what *you* are proactively doing to show that there is so much more out there than just white norms. By showing students original problems, paired with your revised ones, students have opportunities to discuss the inequities prompted by the original problems.

The "condo problem" is an example of a culturally responsive rewrite. The problem was written as, "In a certain condominium community, 2/3 of all the men are married to ¾ of all the women. What fraction of the entire community is married?" As we can see, this problem is inherently flawed. First, in the US, white people are the race owning the most homes (including condos) (National Association of Realtors, 2023). The usage of condos further normalizes home ownership, over renting, which perpetuates white norms. Second, the heterosexual norm of men and women getting married is assumed in this problem, completely disregarding the LGBTQIA+ community. Nabb et al. (2020) worked with teacher candidates to rewrite the problem to be more culturally responsive, and in turn, more approachable, to a larger diversity of students. An example of a revised problem that upholds the mathematical concepts and integrity of the skills being addressed is, "In an apartment building, 2/3rds of the first time renters have dogs. 3/5ths of returning renters have dogs. What fraction of the people in the apartment building have dogs?" Notice the problem is asking for the students to still grapple with proportionality and fractions, using the same numbers, but contextualizes the problem within apartment living, which is much more common in the US across racial communities. The problem also looks at dog ownership, rather than marriage, which could arguably be deemed a missed opportunity to disregard same-sex marriage completely by switching to a dog focus. However, the teacher can show both problems and point out the flaws from the first, to open the discussion so it is not lost completely. As Nabb et al. (2020) summarize, "PK–12 classroom teachers should share with their students the outward tensions that come with situations that expose the systemic structures of privilege and power." As uncomfortable as it may be, explicit instruction about inequities is unavoidable if real change is sought.

I can remember the math problems I had in school and the ones that were included in the curriculum I was given as a public school teacher. Word problems were so mundane and lacked any sort of creativity. Typically, these problems were about two characters buying something, sharing something, trying to get somewhere by a certain time, etc. Like, Billy and Judy buying oranges at the store and having $5 for a bag that costs $4.37 and students needing to figure out how much change they would receive to show they know how to subtract using decimals. I feel like math word problems are a lost opportunity by textbook companies. Most math curricula are written and edited by white people, and it shows. Couldn't math problems be used as a platform for sharing something about another part of the world, another culture, or simply, another race? Seriously, math is used in way more contexts and places than just Billy and Judy at the supermarket getting oranges. Let's bring reality to math problems, to also communicate that students may actually use what we are teaching them in the real world. What about Leilani and Javon being at the store? Such a simple tweak normalizes names that are less common in white culture. Or how about word problems that highlight different ethnic foods, like plantains instead of oranges? What if the supermarket was a "bodega" or a "souk"? See how these changes destabilize the white norms and even encourage students to ask questions to learn more about something that is unfamiliar to them.

Math problems are also an opportunity to recognize that families face different financial challenges. What if instead of every problem being about dollars, we used food stamps and EBT funds to reflect what some families use for payment? What if other currencies are highlighted from around the world? As a faculty member in educator preparation, I work with teacher candidates to write math problems based on literature because starting a math lesson with a book serves as a powerful engagement tool. As explored in the previous chapter, there are a myriad of incredible books that highlight race, racism, equity, and a variety of cultures. Books that kick off math lessons don't need to be books about math or as I like to say, "they don't need to be mathy" to tie into a math lesson. They can be picture books or chapter books. Newhouse (2018) shares how a teacher used "novel study" in pre-algebra to increase student engagement and student investment in both literacy and math. Those students who love to read, but hate math, suddenly see math as more desirable because an area of strength and interest is highlighted.

I use the book *The Name Jar* by Yangsook Choi as an example with my teacher candidates. This book doesn't present math problems and doesn't even have numbers embedded in the text. Haven't heard of it? In short, it's the story of a young girl from Korea who moves to America and is starting at a new school. She is nervous that her name is different and hard for Americans to pronounce, so she considers choosing a more "American" name from a glass jar to better fit in. The story addresses her journey to embrace who she is and her racial and cultural identity. Even though this story doesn't have numbers throughout, it can still be used to write thoughtful, deep, critical math problems for students while also addressing ideas surrounding race.

The key to these problems is to not have the problem simply focus on just any part of the book, but rather, specifically around race, equity, and unique cultural characteristics as explicitly as possible. The problem that I write addresses the Massachusetts Curriculum Framework of "Understand that 10 can be thought of as a bundle of ten ones—called a ten which is for first grade"

(Massachusetts Department of Elementary and Secondary Education [MA DESE], 2017). The problem I show to students is:

> Unhei is self-conscious about her name because people in America struggle to pronounce it correctly. The name is a combination of letters and sounds that are not common in traditional American names. We don't have many names that begin with U. If we wrote down all of the first names of everyone in our class, how many start with each letter of the alphabet. For example, how many names start with "A?" How many names start with "B?"

This problem clearly addresses the idea that someone from another culture could be self-conscious when Americans don't say their name correctly, which provides the opportunity to open the conversation further about pronunciations of names. Such a problem could lead to talking with students about how to politely ask someone to say their name to avoid saying it completely wrong and causing the person to correct the pronunciation (a common microaggression that can be evaded). For older students, a conversation on this topic could go in the direction of addressing assimilation, where the cultural expectation is for BIPOC to try their hardest to silence their cultural and racial identities as much as possible to fit into the white status quo. Such assimilation and the stereotypes of Asian American successes academically and professionally have cast this myth in many Americans' minds that since Asian Americans have thrived in the US, by immigrating over and "pulling themselves up by their bootstraps," then other minoritized groups should be able to do the same (Blackburn, 2019). Students would benefit from learning about why the "model minority myth" is so detrimental. The myth "erases the differences among individuals" and "ignores the diversity of Asian American cultures" along with making white people feel like racism isn't so bad if Asian Americans can achieve so much and it can also pit minoritized races against one another, rather than focusing on the central goal of universal racial equity. In addition, the myth "operates alongside the myth of Asian Americans as perpetual foreigners" and "erases racism against Asian Americans." In such a short problem, such rich discussion can evolve.

Math and Science Investigations That Highlight Racism

The numbers don't lie, as you saw earlier in this book. Racism is not an issue of the past, especially in the field of education. We discussed how statistics can be a powerful tool for convincing others that racism is an issue that needs attention today. This section will look at how quantitative data can be used to address academic standards (i.e., Common Core and Next Generation Science Standards) while also addressing antiracism. The Common Core State Standards (CCSS) have "Measurement and Data" as a recurring category for each grade level, and the Next Generation Science Standards (NGSS) have "analyzing and interpreting data" as an expectation throughout but closely tied to very science-heavy topics. Let's now consider how we may use these standards as leverage to explore race and racism to further cultivate antiracism in our students.

Starting with the math standards from the CCSS, "Measurement and Data" along with other standards provide students with opportunities to not just look at fake example data but real numbers that represent real issues. For example, for third grade, there is the subcategory of "represent and interpret data" and one of the requirements is, "Draw a scaled picture graph and a scaled bar graph to represent a data set with several categories" and students are asked to solve multi-step problems by using the data (CCSS, 2010, p. 25). What if students were given a set of data about income averages for households based on race? They could graph these numbers for the most recent year or for the past several years to notice trends. Such data would show that Asian Americans consistently are the highest earning population, followed by white, non-Hispanic people (Peter G. Peterson Foundation, 2022). The lowest earners are, and have been, black Americans. What an enriching conversation can transpire with this information with students! Together, the class can grapple with questions like, "What is enabling Asian Americans to make the most?" and "Why are black people consistently making the least on average?" This also serves as a paramount opportunity to discuss averages with students to communicate that this data can't lead to assumptions for individuals. In short, just because a person is black, doesn't necessarily mean they are making less money. The key here is "average." There are people whose incomes fall above and below these numbers in every racial category. Being overly reliant on averages can promote stereotypes, which is another conversation worth having with students.

Data analysis and interpretation can also be a great opportunity to discuss "skewed data representation." When I taught fifth grade in 2016, I was a brave soul and decided to teach the presidential election. From the drama of Hilary Clinton's emails to Donald Trump's toxic rhetoric, students were eager to have a space to discuss what they were seeing on the news, hearing on the radio, and absorbing from their parents' conversations. I actually ended up being the only teacher I knew of, in my entire district, who was willing to teach the election, which led to a newspaper visit to highlight my Socratic Seminar teaching methodology. When teaching the election, I heard students quoting a variety of media outlets and even referring to graphs they saw on TV and online. I was intrigued, so we pulled some of these graphs up on my laptop and we looked at them together on the projection screen. They would be polls regarding candidate viability. What was interesting was that based on the political leaning of the news station, the data would make their favored party look more viable. For example, graphs from the conservative-leading station often looked consistently more favorable for Republicans. In contrast, graphs from more liberal news stations would show similar data but more favorable for Democrats. This led to conversations about "skewing data" to show what you want to show. Simply by using different scales on the axes, news stations could make races look close, or like a runaway. We then would talk about what they mean for voters and the impact of peoples' actions when hearing and seeing this information.

Talking about the election inherently addressed race. We looked at data regarding voter racial affiliation and primary numbers to interpret trends and brainstormed why those trends might be taking place. Conversations around policies and issues tied to each candidate's platform helped substantiate these discussions. So, whether it be a presidential election, or a local race, politics can be a great platform for data analysis and discussing social justice issues. Remember, students of all ages are going to talk about politics. It's up to you whether you're going to make space for it to happen with your structure, support, and academic integrations, or if you'd rather them discuss it on the school bus or playground. And that's something to remind parents about, too, in case they show resistance.

Personally, I find math to be easier to integrate antiracism into my teaching than in science. For example, standards about data analysis feel very open-ended and there are always statistics available to make a point clear to students. Science standards, on the other hand, sometimes feel restrictive by often giving a topic and skill at the same time. Science, in my experience, is challenging when integrating antiracism, but not impossible. A helpful guiding idea is that more flexibility in the topic increases approachability. My interpretation of NGSS is that they don't offer many opportunities to apply scientific learning skills to current events and ideas about race, but I did find some that leave room for opportunity. For example, the third-grade standard of "3-LS3-2. Use evidence to support the explanation that traits can be influenced by the environment" could lead to conversations about why people from different parts of the world look different (NGSS, 2017, p. 20). It takes some patience and creativity, but it is possible to make such direct connections.

I find starting with topics to be the most approachable tactic. Science lessons provide opportunities to look closely at a variety of topics and processes and then zoom out to look at systemic injustices and disparities. One example is having students explore the chemistry of taste (Barack, 2021). The scientific nitty-gritty can be the focus at first, but then the discussion can transcend to what foods cause different tastes, then leading to where certain foods are accessible. Inaccessibility can be a point of discussion, and students may read and discuss the problems associated with food deserts and how people largely in BIPOC communities struggle to have fresh, healthy, unprocessed foods. As science educators, we know the value of having students see the societal impacts for research findings and conversations about racism certainly can be a part of this integral step of contextualizing science into everyday lives and systems.

Environmental justice is a topic worth exploring with students, which is, "Environmental justice is the fair treatment and meaningful involvement of all people regardless of race, color, national origin, or income, with respect to the development, implementation, and enforcement of environmental laws, regulations, and policies" (Environmental Protection Agency, 2023). The goal of fair treatment is achieved when all people experience the same level of protection from health and environmental hazards, and everyone has equal access to be a part of the decision-making process to have a healthy environment. In the US, air pollution and climate change are disproportionately affecting BIPOC communities more than white communities (Educators for Social Change, n.d.). It is of paramount importance to teach students about these issues so that they can make informed decisions as citizens for fair treatment for all. One idea for a lesson plan addressing environmental justice would be to uncover how pollution affects low-income communities and minoritized groups by using maps of residential areas that are affected by pollution (Educators for Social Change, n.d.). Environmental racism can inspire service-learning opportunities where students can support communities outside of their own. A word of caution, though: it's important to frame service-learning as one of listening to what other communities need, not stepping in and telling them what they need. This is one step toward avoiding white saviorism.

Exposing students to scientific racism can lead to very insightful discussions with students. Scientific racism is "an organized system of misusing science to promote false scientific beliefs in which dominant racial and ethnic groups are perceived as being superior" (Bonham, 2023). Viewing science through a historical lens is a powerful method for exposing students to the fact that the field of science was used as a tool for promoting racism in the US. For example, in the 1800s, "polygenism" was a theory that different human races were separate species (Harvard Library, 2023). This was based on human skull measurements to falsely argue that the white race was superior. By the late 1800s, scientists showed ridiculous studies in which they claimed that black Americans were more prone to disease and en route toward extinction. Astoundingly, it wasn't until the mid-1900s when scientists disproved these racist "findings." Conversations and explorations around biological investigations of race have the potential to be platforms for learning about how race was invented by society to benefit powerholders, not a biological construct.

When teaching how to be a researcher and follow the scientific method, we talk about biases in our students and how it's important to limit our biases as much as possible to let the data "do the talking." And not have our own opinions corrupt the data. Examples of biases in studies tied to race highlight systemic racism quite well. For example, in the mid-1900s, studies were showing how US prisons were disproportionately black (Harvard Library, 2023). Such a trend was used as the basis for the argument that black people are more prone to commit crimes, thus, yet again, leading to the false claim that white people are superior. The researcher biases were so strong that they blinded them from accounting for poverty, unstable housing, insufficient healthcare, and systemic racism embedded in society. It was studies like these that helped justify more systemic racism, like segregation.

Scientific racism is still happening today. One of the most salient examples is in the medical field. A nursing textbook was pulled in 2017 because it presented racialized stereotypes regarding how certain groups respond to medicine and treatments. This text's messaging is in alignment with a 2015 article that showed how white medical school students tend to falsely believe that black people have a lower pain toleration, leading to lower treatment rates for black people (Hoffman et al., 2016). It is important that students know that scientific racism is still happening and they can play a role in ending it by starting with addressing four points of understanding to eliminate any ideas the race has bearing on one's achievement: (1) people are not born with outstanding talents, (2) racism in society is not "just natural," (3) certain groups don't just naturally excel in particular domains (like athletics), and (4) no one race is more prone to higher or lower IQs (ASM, 2023). *Real* studies that address race, but not in a racist way, should be shown or discussed with students so that they can see that race can be a part of research, without being detrimental to groups. An example of this could be a study about sickle cell anemia and how "those who were forcibly enslaved were from geographic regions where skin pigmentation protected from UV damage and explain how this correlated with regions where malaria is endemic and a mutation in a single beta-globin allele offered protection against malaria" (ASM, 2023). Remember that genetic ancestry cannot be used interchangeably with race. The only time that race can be used to look at health outcomes is when seeing the role racism has on people's health. Educators, let's use examples of scientific racism to inspire future scientists who will use their knowledge to provide evidence that moves society toward equity, not further derision.

Looking Ahead: The Future of Math and Science

This chapter has provided ideas, strategies, questions, and reflections that at times may have "revved your engine" and at other times, made you feel overwhelmed by bringing antiracism to your math and science instruction. I never said it was easy, and I acknowledge these are not the most approachable and user-friendly domains for this work, but it is very doable and necessary. Imagine you revamp your ELA and social studies lessons with lots of antiracist themes, ideas, and discussions and totally disregard these topics in math and science. Consider what messaging that sends to students. Does it communicate that white-centered norms in math and science are acceptable? Does it disregard the whiteness of those fields completely? Yes, to both. Math and science, while maybe the least clear-cut to make antiracist, warrant more of your time and attention to ensure they are not forgotten so that antiracism is threaded throughout your entire day with students to further communicate the necessary pervasiveness of antiracism for it to be effective.

Before moving into reflective questions, I wish to leave you with a powerful outlook into the future for math and science. Song (2020) summarized changes that she contends as necessarily for the future of math education, which I have adapted below for both math and science. I think they align beautifully with the work we are doing in this book.

1. Math and science achievement won't be used as a means to further oppress marginalized groups through high-stakes testing. Rather, such assessments will be used as tools for bringing humanity back to classrooms.
2. Math and science curricula will shift to address community issues, explore them, and brainstorm solutions while challenging societal norms that carry the toxic status quo of white supremacy.
3. Teachers of math and science will be prepared to talk about race, power dynamics, marginalization, and other societal issues and know how to support students in navigating those challenges.

All these aspirations for the future are obtainable with your voice and your actions at the helm.

Dr. McGowan Weighs In

As noted in this chapter, representation matters when teaching mathematics and science to elementary school students, especially in classrooms that are majority or all white. It is important to refer to historical and current representation. Many school districts engage in blood drives which is an excellent opportunity to have a discussion about Dr. Charles Richard Drew and his contributions on how hospitals and other facilities store blood. It is also a great opportunity to have books and visual representations of contemporary women scientists. I am thinking of Vanessa Wyche who is the current African American director of the NASA Johnson Space Center.

Reflective Questions

I now invite you to reflect on the ideas presented in this chapter.

1. What images and examples have you provided students of mathematicians and scientists? How could you improve upon these?
2. Look at the example problems you supply your students in your math curriculum. Do they perpetuate only white cultural norms? If so, how could they be improved and what are your next steps in doing so?
3. Review the math standard(s) that you cover in the course of the year specifically addressing data analysis. How do you plan to address this standard, or multiple standards, by using data that is race-based? What types of meaningful conversations would you endeavor to host with your students?
4. Can you find a math standard that isn't focused on data analysis that could connect to race and equity? How would you structure a lesson with this focus?
5. What avenues could you pursue to communicate systemic racism to students? How can you highlight students' roles in fighting it through math and science?
6. Take a look at your science standards that have some openness about the topics. How could race place a role in any of those? What topics connected directly to racial justice that you could explore further with students?
7. How do you think you could approach the topic of scientific racism with your students?
8. Since exploring race in math and science means that lessons may take longer, due to deep discussions and reflections, how receptive is your school's principal to that fact? For instance, if you're teaching a math lesson and using statistics to explore environmental racism, and students have lots of examples and questions, which delay you starting the activity/assignment and you need to finish the next day, which throws off your curricular pacing a bit, is that deemed acceptable where you teach?

Or is the curricular pacing rigidity too strict to make that okay? If it's not okay, what is your course of action for sticking to pacing, without sacrificing integrations of racial topics in math and science?
9. Pick a book from your classroom library that addresses a concept of race and/or racial equity. Now, pick a math standard that you need to address in an upcoming lesson. Can you write a math problem that highlights an idea about race or equity, then delve into the math? Try it out!

References

American Society for Microbiology (2023, May 10). Addressing scientific racism and eugenics in the classrooms. https://asm.org/Articles/2023/May/Addressing-Scientific-Racism-and-Eugenics-in-the-C

Associated Press (2020, June 25). Census shows white decline, nonwhite majority among youngest Americans. *NBC News*. https://www.nbcnews.com/news/us-news/census-shows-white-decline-nonwhite-majority-among-youngest-americans-n1232094

Barack, L. (2021, May 26). Weaving antibias and equity into curricula begins with self-reflection. *K-12 Dive*. https://www.k12dive.com/news/weaving-anti-bias-and-equity-into-curricula-begins-with-self-reflection/600681/

Blackburn, S. (2019, March 21). What is the model minority myth? Learning for Justice. https://www.learningforjustice.org/magazine/what-is-the-model-minority-myth

Bonham, V. L., Jr. (2023, June 20). Scientific racism. *The Human Genome Research Institute*. https://www.genome.gov/genetics-glossary/Scientific-Racism

Common Core State Standards Initiative (2010). *Common core state standards for mathematics*. https://learning.ccsso.org/wp-content/uploads/2022/11/Math_Standards1.pdf

Educators for Social Change (n.d.). Teaching for environmental justice. *United for Social Change*. https://educators4sc.org/teaching-about-environmental-justice/

Environmental Protection Agency (2023, May 12). *Environmental racism*. https://www.epa.gov/environmentaljustice

Gay, G. (2018). *Culturally responsive teaching: Theory, research, and practice.* New York: Teachers College Press.

Harvard Library (2023). *Scientific racism.* https://library.harvard.edu/confronting-anti-black-racism/scientific-racism

Hoffman, K. M., Trawalter, S., Axt, J. R., & Oliver, M. N. (2016, Apr. 4). Racial bias in pain assessment and treatment recommendations, and false beliefs about biological differences between blacks and whites. *Proceedings of the National Academy of Sciences, 113*(16), 4296–4301. https://doi.org/10.1073/pnas.1516047113

Johnson, S. R. (2022, Nov. 16). US News—Harris poll survey: As America aims for equity, many believe systemic racism doesn't exist. *US News.* https://www.usnews.com/news/health-news/articles/2022-11-16/poll-many-americans-dont-believe-systemic-racism-exists

Massachusetts Department of Elementary and Secondary Education (2017). *Mathematics grades pre-Kindergarten to 12: Massachusetts curriculum framework –2017.* https://www.doe.mass.edu/frameworks/math/2017-06.pdf

Nabb, K., Murawska, J., Doty, J., Fredlund, A., Hofer, S., McAllister, C., Miller, S., Nassif, Z., Pearson, S., Pike-Nobile, A., & Welch, E. (2020). The condo problem: Is this culturally responsive teaching? *Mathematics Teacher: Learning and Teaching PK-12 MTLT, 113*(9), 692–701. https://doi.org/10.5951/MTLT.2019.0400

National Association of Realtors (2023, March 2). *More Americans own their homes, but Black-White homeownership rate gap is biggest in a decade, NAR report finds.* https://www.nar.realtor/newsroom/more-americans-own-their-homes-but-black-white-homeownership-rate-gap-is-biggest-in-a-decade-nar

Newhouse, K. (2018, Mar. 18). How reading novels in math class can strengthen student engagement. *KQED.* https://www.kqed.org/mindshift/50640/how-reading-novels-in-math-class-can-strengthen-student-engagement

Next Generation Science Standards (2017). *Topic arrangements of the next generation science standards.* https://www.nextgenscience.org/sites/default/files/AllTopic.pdf

Peter C. Peterson Foundation (2022, Nov. 9). *Income and wealth in the United States: An overview of recent data.* https://www.pgpf.org/blog/2023/02/income-and-wealth-in-the-united-states-an-overview-of-recent-data

Song, E. (2020). Now: The future of mathematics education. Mathematics Teacher: Learning and Teaching PK-12, *113*(12), 1044–1045. https://doi.org/10.5951/MTLT.2020.0150

US Office of Federal Operations (2019). Special topics annual report: Women in STEM. *US Equal Employment Opportunity Commission.* https://www.eeoc.gov/special-topics-annual-report-women-stem

8

Social Studies/Civics Approaches

One Teacher's Experience Mirroring a National Trend

When I was a fifth-grade teacher, I didn't inherit a social studies curriculum of any sort. I was shown the MA curriculum frameworks for history and social sciences and was told to teach this subject when I could but to try and not take too much time dedicated to it because it wasn't addressed in the fifth-grade round of state testing. English Language Arts (ELA), math, and science needed to always be the priority. This is a norm nationwide. RAND researchers found that on average, the typical elementary student experiences nine hours on ELA, seven hours on math, three hours on science, and three hours on social studies, every week (Will, 2023). In a nation that wants students to thrive in reading, I find it a bit baffling that when research shows improved literacy is linked to increased social studies instructional time, we don't mark this discipline with more prioritization. Social studies helping literacy makes sense, though. If students have improved background knowledge, they better understand what they read (i.e., reading comprehension). The lack of social studies instruction is missing just as much in teacher development as well. Only 52% of elementary principals reported that teachers received some sort of support for their social studies instruction during the 2021–2022 academic year (Will, 2023). Learning opportunities and coaching for ELA and math were twice as common, though. Also, the more poverty in a school district, the less focus on social studies (Will, 2023), which clearly indicates that social studies is yet another white privilege because, the higher the poverty, the less white a school is (National Center for Education Statistics, 2023). A dearth of social studies in elementary curricula is telling our youngest learners that it is a subject area that doesn't warrant prioritization (Will, 2023).

As someone whose favorite subject in school growing up was history, I was disheartened by the lack of prioritization of learning about the past when I became a teacher. As a firm believer that understanding the past can prevent nations from repeating past mistakes, I see much value in learning about our country's successes and failures. Our students can learn from this sentiment as well because it speaks to the power of reflection leading to action and progress. The American Historical Association (Stearns, 2020) summarizes why studying history is so important which includes that history (1) helps us understand people and societies and enact change, as well as how the society in which we live came to fruition, (2) connects to our own lives, (3) contributes to our morals, (4) serves as opportunities to work on our identity formation, and (5) develops strong citizenship/civic understanding in people. Learning of the past matters, so I endeavored to make the most of what little time I had each week to dedicate my instruction to social studies.

After scouring my classroom and sorting through the immense amount of stuff that decades of teachers have left behind in this classroom, in the back of the room, at the very bottom of a bookcase, was a bunch of social studies textbooks from the 1980s. They were covered with dust and seemed like they hadn't been used in quite some time. That was my sign that I needed to create my materials myself. In retrospect, while it was a ton of work to craft my own lesson materials for social studies, I'm thankful I wasn't forced to use one of the whitewashed curricula that other teachers are forced to use. I was able to address the standards but fill in the details with truth and honesty with my fifth graders. It was a useful learning opportunity because

I didn't know the answers to plenty of questions I was asked and the amount of research I had to do to put lessons together was immense.

My experience isn't solitary. About a third of elementary principals in the 2021–2022 academic year reported that they didn't offer any social studies curricula to their teachers. Forty percent said they gave publisher-created curricula to teachers. In addition, RAND researchers found 38% of teachers said that they "held the reins" in deciding what and how to teach social studies (Will, 2023). Only 21% of teachers were told what they were teaching and how. ELA and math are different stories. Most teachers said that their districts made decisions and mandated what they use and how they teach ELA and math. Just as I was piecemealing my curricular materials together, other teachers are doing the same today. Research has shown that teachers are largely researching online and purchasing things off "Teachers Pay Teachers" to throw together their best iteration of the past to share (Will, 2023). More professional development and guidance are needed to ensure consistent social studies quality.

As I taught social studies during my first year as a teacher, I quickly picked up on the fact that students' historical insights were lacking. In a general sense, they struggled to know common facts about the past and the establishment of our nation, which is surprising being in Massachusetts where there is a historical landmark related to the establishment of the country around just about every corner. So, we started with the "European explorers" standard I was to address for the state, and at the time, Columbus' savage and disturbing true story was not as commonly discussed. However, I knew this truth and created my own slides and selected my own articles to share with the class to disrupt the "fairytale" that Columbus was so great and should be celebrated. This honest view of the past carried us into the establishment of the 13 original colonies and discussions around slavery. One of the most pivotal moments in my teaching career was when my class of fifth graders looked at me in utter disbelief and disgust that slavery had occurred. I recall saying, "Wait, no one has talked to you about slavery in this nation?" Nope. No one had. To get to 10–11 years old and not know that slavery occurred made my skin crawl. How can these children understand how terrible it is that the same population that was once enslaved in this nation is still actively fighting against overt and covert racism in this country if they don't know slavery happened? Such a huge, ugly aspect of American history needs to be communicated with students transparently or else the racial equity failings of the Reconstruction period after the Civil War, the limitations of the Civil Rights Movement, up through the turbulence of today's Black Lives Matter Movement won't make much sense and not carry nearly the same amount of weight. Providing students with the facts of the past, including the ugly sides of American history, means that we are helping students become informed citizens to enact societal change.

In this chapter, we will unpack what it means to "decolonize" our approach to teaching the past through an un-whitewashed lens in an age-appropriate way, provide insights regarding how teachers can re-educate themselves, share instructional recommendations when using a pre-boxed curriculum, grapple with the idea of national pride in ourselves and help our students through that process, and delve into considerations on how to address civics as a necessary element of social studies. The terms "history" and "social studies" are used interchangeably throughout this chapter, but both are intended to encapsulate historical narratives and the examination of social groups. It is also important to fully recognize that teaching a decolonized view of the past can lead to pushback, so I encourage you to think about the strategies and approaches discussed earlier in this book and apply them to how you would handle resistance to you teaching a more truthful, inclusive version of the past, rooted in facts and evidence.

Decolonizing and Un-Whitewashing Social Studies

You may have seen the terms, "decolonize" and "un-whitewashing" before but didn't fully understand what they mean. Decolonization and un-whitewashing are what drive the curricular and instructional revisions you are making in social studies by being an antiracist teacher. As Lewis says, decolonizing the past is "broadly about making historians aware of and committed to addressing the disproportionate focus on Eurocentric history" rooted in underlying structural powers (Behm et al., 2020, p. 171). Behm adds, "decolonizing history encompasses confronting, examining, and in turn dismantling chauvinist and supremacist ways of knowing and doing history" (Behm et al., 2020, p. 171). There are many throughlines here to "un-whitewashing." In essence, "Whitewashed history leaves out minority and marginalized communities, or hides the truth to make historical situations seem more palatable for white teachers to teach" (Erdman, 2021). Furthermore, "often, the history taught in school leaves out important events and underrepresented communities, or paints an entirely different, whitewashed picture" (Erdman, 2021). In sum, to tell whitewashed narratives of the past means they are inherently colonized. As colonizers were white people, telling a history that centers whiteness means that whitewashing and colonization of history go together. This section will discuss two major areas that can help you consider the content you're hoping to un-whitewash and decolonize. These include revising (1) whose histories we tell and who is silenced and (2) misrepresentations of people and events throughout history.

Whose History Do We Tell and Whose Stories Do We Silence?

When you look at US history textbooks, it is clear that white men are the most prominent figures throughout the text. From European kings sending explorers to far-off lands to the Founding Fathers of America, white men are the primary "heroes." As teachers, it is of the utmost importance that we critically examine whose stories we are telling and in what ways. For example, why are white men always the "knights in shining armor," while People of Color, when they *are* included, are shown as those needing to persevere, survive, experiencing immense struggle, or serving as subservient supporters of a White, male Eurocentric perspective? This common dynamic is problematic for many reasons. What kind of messaging are we passing to our students? It's no wonder that students who identify as white and male are more likely to enjoy history and have high academic achievement in this subject area than their peers who identify as female or part of a minoritized group. Female and minoritized students feel alienated by the narratives in the curricula (Loewen, 2018). The Eurocentric views cast upon the reader make the "we" and "us" of the textbooks exclusionary for students of color in particular. A truly multicultural text would make all readers uncomfortable at points, not just those who don't fit the heroic figures represented the most. White men did some terrible things and there are incredible success stories for People of Color, all of which have been told as footnotes or "fun facts" readers need to find out on their own.

While we know that white men are pervasively the focus of US history textbooks, Indigenous voices have been largely silenced and restricted to the past, like they aren't around today. Students can't be ignorant of the horrible treatment and mass murders of Indigenous peoples that took place before the pilgrims arrived (i.e., the arrival of explorers like Columbus), and after they arrived. This can start with discussing how Columbus Day should be officially recognized as Indigenous Peoples' Day nationwide and the true story that has sparked this movement. Contact your local tribal community to see if they would be interested in meeting to discuss the curriculum you have and their recommendations for increasing indigeneity in your teaching. They may even provide opportunities for guest speakers and class trips.

For older elementary students, it can be thought-provoking to have students look at the narratives that have been told in schools and the real versions in contrast and ask them, "why do you think the false version was told for so long?" For groups and individual figures who have been silenced, they can think about why those voices haven't been heard. This will inevitably lead to discussions about racism, colonialism, power, and more. Modern-day injustices will inevitably become a talking point.

Misrepresentation of People and Events
If you're mentioned in a US history textbook, you must have done some great things and deserve to be remembered with

admiration and honor, right? Well, not really. Let's take a look at Thomas Jefferson, who is a pretty quintessential example. He was a man filled with contradictions. While publicly denouncing slavery, he enslaved about 600 people in his lifetime and he even made clear that a "multiracial society with free black people was impossible" (Wiencek, 2012). His relationship with his wife's half-sister who was an enslaved maid at Monticello (the plantation he owned and operated), Sally Hemings, has been the grounds of historical intrigue as well. There is strong speculation that she gave birth to six of Jefferson's biological children, all of whom he eventually set free (Monticello.org, n.d.). And this is just the "tip of the iceberg" when it comes to Jefferson's unforgivable misdeeds. When trying to learn more about his past, it's important to look for sources that do not have their own political agenda. Finding sources that just give the facts is key. For example, for this chapter, I read information from "Monticello and the Thomas Jefferson Foundation" and the Smithsonian, sources that just reported the facts without interpretation. I was able to put the facts together to tell me more about what was likely the case about his relationship with Sally Hemings, which was clear to me that it was less than a consensual relationship if you see where I'm going. Not that I get to look at a $2 bill often, but when I do, it certainly is not in high regard for this man anymore.

In an opposite light, historians have villainized Malcolm X. When learning about the Civil Rights Movement, the first name that comes to most peoples' minds is Dr. Martin Luther King, Jr. While MLK's impact was awe-inspiring and should be recalled with admiration, it is often told in a way that overshadows others' contributions. I always get the sense that textbook editors don't want too many People of Colors' voices, so they overcompensate with one, which ensures they don't need to highlight others. Malcolm X was arguably as influential of a figure for black rights; however, his path and his messaging were starkly different than that of Dr. King's. His initial messaging, when speaking as a member of the Nation of Islam, was one of physical defense against white people and encouraged black people to claim their civil rights "by any means necessary" (Associated

Press, 2022). At that point in his career, he and MLK were at odds, due to Malcolm's acceptance of violence as sometimes needed. His messaging changed to one of aspiring to racial unity after he split from the Black Muslim Organization and traveled to Mecca. I personally find Malcolm X to be one of the most inspiring historical figures in racial justice history. He did what so many leaders never do: he changed his mind. He learned, grew, and shifted along with learning. In a world where so many people dig their heels into the ground with their opinions with an unwillingness to reconsider their perspectives, I think we can all learn from Malcolm X, especially our nation's youth. Furthermore, Malcolm's messaging around black people's greatest tool is to be their best selves as a means to help the movement for black rights is powerful, especially with his message about education being such an important tool for bettering oneself (Bartlett, 2015). If this messaging were more well known, couldn't it be useful today?

There are also historical events that have been mischaracterized in history. On a basic level, the first Thanksgiving is a prime example that has led to storybook-like renditions of the relationships between colonizers and Indigenous peoples. But even more recent history is being misrepresented in textbooks. Often, when there is a shameful moment in US history, textbooks will move past it as quickly as possible—just long enough to be able to "check the box" that they covered the topic but not long enough to say too much that may make the reader think poorly of the US. The war in Vietnam is a prime example. Interestingly, textbooks try to include photos from the war to help tell the story, but the photos lack the terror and destruction that was really the epitome of that war (Loewen, 2018). Images aside, the descriptions of the war ignore the fact that the US committed so many disgusting war crimes. The My Lai Massacre is typically described as an isolated incident, but it was one of many similar horrific scenes of the war in Vietnam. What about all the opposition to the Vietnam War? Hard to find books that quote MLK or Muhammad Ali as against the war. Loewen (2018) argues that textbooks should supply the facts and let the reader contemplate critical questions that open controversies to explore. And remarkably, much of the controversies surrounding the war in Vietnam, and history in general, is that there is no solid, right answer. Textbook editors try their hardest to avoid controversy and want to project fallacies of clear-cut storylines and resolutions. The opaque version of the Vietnam War leaves students without helpful insights that could help them make sense of even more recent history (like the war in Iraq) and current events (like the war in Ukraine). In fact, you'll find in textbooks, the more recent the events, the less coverage there is on that content. This is largely because parents of the students reading these books have lived through the recent past and have experiences that could challenge the narratives they write in the books (Loewen, 2018). There are so many benefits of writing about the recent past in detail, like (1) if authors lived through these times, they have more knowledge to share, (2) multiple perspectives are available and can be supported with evidence, and (3) authors can research for themselves and not be so reliant on others (Loewen, 2018). As we consider how we can revise the content we are teaching, it needs to start with re-educating ourselves as teachers.

Teacher Re-education

Previously in this book, we discussed how important it is to do the "self-work" before focusing on professional integrations of antiracism. Simply by reading this chapter, you may have likely already had moments of "I didn't know that!" or "How come no one taught me that when I was in school?" I know that's what I was saying to myself when I started my US history re-education process. When I first started, I was honestly a bit frustrated by the amount of relearning I had to do to be a better teacher. First, I had to learn all the new ways to teach math due to more conceptual methods being employed and then I realized that much of the historical narratives I thought were standard were deeply flawed and harmful. If teachers are going to craft lessons that are more truthful and inclusive, then they need to know whose stories have been silenced and who has been over-glorified. That background knowledge serves as a strong foundation to then be able to make instructional decisions as to what curricula and textbooks are helping or harming their students' learning.

Something that helped me on my journey of relearning the past was to first realize that my relearning is not my way of promoting "revisionist history." This idea of spreading "revisionist history" has become a widely popular conservative argument. Those people claim that when individuals are uncovering wrongdoings of America's past and sharing it with others, those individuals are rewriting the past to make the US look terrible (Bracken et al., 2022). In actuality, the storybook version of the nation's past that makes everything look rosy and dandy is "revisionist" because it simply is rooted in lies and ignores the truth. So when conservatives have cried out that they are against "revisionist history," they are promoting their own "revisionist history." What I was trying to do was undo the perceptions and understandings cemented in my mind that were through decades of learning the storybook version that inundated my school experiences. It was book authors and editors that were "re-envisioning" the past. I just needed the true facts to interpret those insights myself.

I found James Loewen's (2018) book, *Lies My Teacher Told Me: Everything Your American History Textbook Got Wrong* as a seminal text for guidance. He explains why textbooks have been so whitewashed and gives powerful summaries of aspects of the past that have been grotesquely, inaccurately told in public education. His succinct explanations have led me down research rabbit holes to get more details regarding the nuggets he shares. This is the type of book you can read multiple times and every time, something new will stand out to you that is worth exploring further on your own.

Loewen (2018) taught me about historiography, which is the study of how history is told. Textbooks are typically tertiary sources, meaning they are laden with interpretations. Loewen explains the power of primary sources in allowing ourselves and our students to interpret the past for ourselves. Just give the facts, the documents, and the photos, and see what happens.

When given these materials, the storybook narratives that are so popular in American textbooks seem strangely misconstrued. With a list of facts about Thomas Jefferson's past, how could he be heroized as the one who stated, "All men are created equal?" Let's consider looking at primary source documents to help us make our own interpretations of the past.

Using primary and secondary source documents doesn't mean that tertiary sources aren't an integral part of the process as well. I mean, as teachers, do you really have the time to delve into primary source documents every day and record your interpretations? No. However, they can be helpful when paired with vetted texts that can debunk historical over-glorifications and silenced stories. Paired with James Loewen's book, I found Ibram X. Kendi's (2017) *Stamped from the Beginning: The Definitive History of Racist Ideas in America* as a necessary guide to help me understand the history of racism in this country specifically. And there are versions of this book for a variety of age levels, because the original text would be unapproachable for younger readers (but beneficial to your own learning). It's a big book, which I enjoyed as an audiobook, and I recommend it. As you go through your process of relearning, you may be considering how you'll bring these ideas to your teaching. Well, Kendi's got you covered with his other versions of the book.

The 1619 Project from the genius of Nikole Hannah-Jones has been incredibly useful to the teacher candidates I teach and myself. The New York Times offers educational tools and I especially like the podcast episodes, as they truly bring the history to life. The impetus of the project is to provide a "new origin story for the United States, one that helped explain not only the persistence of anti-Black racism and inequality in American life today, but also the roots of so much of what makes the country unique" (1619 Books, 2023). The approachable way that Hannah-Jones has curated the information makes it a useful resource for us and students.

Remember how earlier in this book we talked about identifying your biases and using them as opportunities for further learning? Think about those biases as inspiration for learning about history, too. For example, as uncomfortable as it is to admit, I knew I had a bias against East Asian and Pacific Islanders because I previously thought they all looked alike and knew very little about the variety of countries from which these people came. While learning about their cultures has been hugely helpful, looking at these populations through a historical lens has been enlightening, too. I have felt prompted to research East Asian and Pacific Islanders in American history and the US role in that part of the world. This has led me down some dark roads of research, which I'm glad I now know more about because it helps me understand and have an active voice against modern-day prejudices.

As you craft a list of resources for your own learning and pull together materials for your students, Loewen (2018) encourages the following questions to increase the critical engagement with the sources. These include (1) When and by whom was it written? (2) Whose viewpoint is presented primarily? (3) Would you say the narrative is believable, or are you left with skepticism? (4) Is the narrative supported by other sources? and (5) How are you left feeling about how America is presented? Take these considerations into how you critically examine the boxed curriculum you might be asked to use in your teaching.

Using a Pre-boxed Curriculum and Adding in the Truth

This subsection will discuss how teachers can follow district guidelines by using the curriculum they are given but use it as a basis for supplementing the true details that students need to know. I fully understand that our readership from the southern states that are facing much stricter guidelines may read this and think it is not for them. However, I will review some strategies that could still help you find those "nuggets" of flexibility within the rigid structures they are up against.

Doyle and Doyle (2020) summarized the work of historians Fred Anderson and Andrew Cayton. They contend that school textbooks are based largely on "three 'good wars for freedom'" (Doyle & Doyle, 2020). These include "The Revolutionary War birthing Americans' commitment to liberty; the Civil War extending freedom to enslaved people; World War II exporting American freedom worldwide—so goes the sanitized classroom (and Hollywood) story" (Doyle & Doyle, 2020). If a war happened but doesn't carry a message of the US serving as the "good guys of freedom," it's mentioned in passing, if not glossed over completely. Examples include Vietnam, Korea, Spanish-America, and the countless conflicts against Indigenous peoples. Wars—all wars—are an opportunity for students to explore the imperialism and expansionism that motivated the fighting. Ignoring these ideas leads to "hyper-patriotic narratives" that need serious rewriting (Doyle & Doyle, 2020). Interestingly though, this is what we get in K–12 textbooks, even though scholars have researched narratives that are more inclusive versions of the past that are not exuding exceptionalism. Doyle and Doyle (2020) argue that it is wise for primary and secondary teachers who want to reform their history curricula to partner with academic historians. They can help fill in areas that are missing or false in curricula.

Leslie Mac, an antiracist organizer, emphasizes that being an antiracist takes action and that teachers have a responsibility to take action when injustice is present. Accepting and not resisting these absurd accounts of US history is a missed opportunity to live antiracist ideals (Doyle & Doyle, 2020). White educators must not just read the books and have private conversations. They need to share the truths so students can spark change, not just keep repeating past mistakes.

Interestingly, even if teachers themselves identify differently politically, or are of different races, a common theme is to supply students with the facts and let them make sense of what they are presented (Bracken et al., 2022). The questions in history textbooks are typically mind-numbing and reliant upon being able to find the answers in the books themselves (Loewen, 2018). What about open-ended questions that don't lead to straightforward answers? Those types of questions can feel uncomfortable to use as teachers, but they spark higher order thinking and greater engagement with the content. Teaching history needs to be less about memorization and more about making sense of facts and having more questions than answers. History is filled with controversy and students should know this and learn that not all questions will be answered firmly. And this isn't just an approach for older students. Telling simple, false stories to younger students isn't acceptable because lying is a slippery slope. Once you start, when do you stop? Like, does third-grade roll around and as the teacher you must revisit what they were taught and unpack the truth? Talk about confusion for those students! So, for readers teaching the early elementary grades, consider how you can tell the truth but make it approachable for younger students. This can be as simple as telling of the Pilgrims landing and stealing land that wasn't theirs. Students can relate to this and feel an emotional connection to it because they likely have had times when someone takes something of theirs. In fact, emotion can serve as a means to get students to remember the history they learn (Loewen, 2018).

Moving forward, it's useful to reflect upon James Loewen's points he recommends teachers consider:

1. Examine fewer topics but with greater depth.
2. Don't feel pressured to know it all; learn alongside your students.
3. Encourage students to use their family's knowledge and local history (like Indigenous voices, for example).
4. Experiment with teaching history backward to prompt connection-making between history and the present.

Grappling with "National Pride"

When learning the "ugly" side of American history, it can be easy to feel ashamed of the country's past. I, myself, have struggled to feel "proud to be an American" when I learn about the terrible things that this country has done to a variety of groups of people of varying backgrounds. The summer I read Kendi's *Stamped from the Beginning,* I abstained from my usual Fourth of July festivities. I was processing my American identity and how I felt about being born and raised in the country with such a horrific past and still struggling with many of the same issues. I felt like I was going through a bit of a grieving process for the country I thought I knew. I had been aware of many blemishes in the nation's story, the more I learned, the heavier my heart became. How could one country cause so much death, pain, destruction, and lasting ramifications on such a wide scale? How could a country end slavery but still have racism so rampant? To be honest, I got into a bit of a negative spiral about America. It didn't help that American pride was associated politically with conservatives (I'm liberal, if you haven't guessed), so wearing the stars and stripes and singing "My Country Tis of Thee" wasn't coming as natural anymore. However, rather than continuing to spiral, I chose to reflect on my "national pride journey" by reading, writing, and discussing these ideas and sentiments with anyone who would listen. This process taught me that I can define my own definition of "national pride," which means it doesn't need to be politically rooted or disregard the hard truths of the past. My own definition of national pride can be one of optimism and hope. Here's where I landed: I am proud to be an American because I come from a nation that is unlike any other with the beautiful medley of people it has in it. America is an experiment that is constantly twisting, turning, and shifting. It goes through ups and downs, but what makes me proud is the *potential* of America. America has the potential to be a nation of people of all colors, gender identities, sexual orientations, spiritualities, abilities, birth nations, and languages that can live in harmony and celebrate differences. The potential is there. Will I see it to full fruition in my lifetime? Certainly not. But will it get better for every generation? I'm confident it will because I think that's the trajectory we are on. And while news of *Roe vs. Wade* overturned and the ending of affirmative action for college admissions feel like steps backward, those types of misguided actions are going to happen along the way. The path of progress is never straightforward and if we want the progress to last and be deep-rooted, it must be challenging and have some steps backward. I think a key part to this authentic change of the nation needs to be reflective in nature, which involves a clear understanding of this nation's past mistakes.

As students learn about their nation, and all its mistakes and wrongdoings, some students may need time to process their own perspectives and emotions about the country. Some may even feel like they do not want to partake in everyday routines rooted in nationalism, like singing patriotic songs or standing for the Pledge of Allegiance. The phrase "Liberty and Justice for All" is arguably a future ambition, not the current status, and students may need time to think about that. Also, students may feel uncomfortable with the pledge because they may not religiously align with the phrase, "under God." In fact, that phrase wasn't added until 1954, during the Cold War, when Congress wanted to emphasize how the US was so different from the atheist Soviet Union (Criss, 2019). Consider letting students know that your classroom is a safe and brave space to talk about the pledge and to let them know that standing is a personal decision and that in your classroom, their decision will be respected. They should know that the Constitution doesn't state that students are mandated to stand (Criss, 2019). In fact, forcing a student to stand is against their First Amendment rights. Fostering this safe and brave space is also an integral part of students to learn about their civic duties as citizens.

Civics Education as an Essential Part of Social Studies

Civics can be defined as, "the study or science of the privileges and obligations of citizens" (League of Women Voters of Delaware, n.d.). Civic life is seen as essential to democracy. Rates of young people engaging civically are declining. This is seen in statistics like 25% of Americans not being able to name the three branches of government. And in rural areas, 60% of youth live in "civic deserts," which means they lack opportunities to convene to talk about problems and issues. And since rural schools are often predominantly white, this means that white students aren't being civically engaged. Reasons for youth not being civically engaged range "from political dysfunction to an actively polarized media to the growing mobility of Americans and even the technological transformation of leisure" (Winthrop, 2020). Schools can play a vital part in emphasizing civics in youth lives.

In 42 states and D.C., they require at least one civics course for students before graduating from 12th grade, but only 11 states require some sort of civic education *experience* (Winthrop, 2020). And these courses are typically at the secondary level. The focus in schools had been increasingly centered on reading, math, and science, as seen in the tests that are given. And the academic push here is with the ambition to make the US more economically competitive. I find this interesting, since business leaders claim that they need employees who are academically competent but also have the skills to lead teams, communicate effectively with partners, come up with new ways to solve problems, and effectively navigate an increasingly digital world. And while the 21st Century Skills Movement emphasizes social skills, "they do not explicitly impart strong norms and values about society" (Winthrop, 2020). So are 21st Century Skills really addressing the civic-related qualities that business leaders desire in employees?

With the social unrest that is still very present in this nation, civic education serves an important purpose. Louise Dubé states that when "we educate young people about how we can make change and come together for the common good" that is when "we teach the knowledge, skills, and dispositions to solve civic issues by engaging across differences" (Coleman-Mortley, 2020). A huge part of civic education is having students learn to stand up for justice and accept others' inputs, even if they look different than them. Remember how in Chapter 6 we talked about communicating with students the message that they can be change-makers? Civics education aligns with that sentiment. Civics takes learning and considers how it can benefit society through practical actions by everyday citizens. Civics is so important to learning about the past because it's the "now what?" part that inspires implementation for change.

How can teachers bring these skills to their practice? High-quality civics education has shown to lead to increased civic engagement by students, meaning they use what they learn in the real world (Winthrop, 2020). Service-learning on community projects that partner with organizations and extracurricular activities where students work as teams is a good start. Simulations of democratic procedures, establishing and participating in a school government, and contributing to school climate initiatives are also worth consideration. The C3 (College, Career, and Civic Life) Standards are guiding principles for social studies education and are intended to (1) address the marginalization of social studies, (2) motivate students to influence the real world, and (3) integrate civics education to benefit our democracy so students leave school knowing about their civic duties (National Council for the Social Studies, n.d.). The C3 Framework has four dimensions, including (1) developing questions and planning inquiries, (2) applying disciplinary tools and concepts, (3) evaluating sources and using evidence, and (4) communicating conclusions and taking informed action. By addressing these dimensions, civics, economics, geography and history can be covered.

As we consider our roles as white teachers of white students, teaching the past through a decolonized, un-whitewashed lens is an integral part of inspiring students that this nation has a history of flaws that can teach us so much moving forward. Disregarding the past out of fear of developing some disdain for America's actions is not enough of a reason to forfeit an invaluable learning opportunity. Understanding the past, paired with skills and motivation to bring this knowledge to their roles as citizens means that as teachers, we are equipping these students to spur societal change. Ignorance is a dangerous thing that US textbooks have been perpetuating for generations and as antiracist educators, it can stop with us.

Dr. McGowan Weighs In

As we talk about American History, social studies, and civic education, it is important to remind readers that throughout history, People of Color actively fought against enslavement, decolonization, and racism in all of its manifestations. It is also important to be mindful of how People of Color currently fight to disrupt individual, institutional, and systemic racism relative to history, social studies, and civics education. Growing up in my African American community, I remember heated debates about how we as African Americans should not celebrate July 4th. As someone born and raised in Houston, Texas, I also remember discussions about celebrating Juneteenth as our liberation day instead of July 4th. As I reflect on those conversations, I feel that it is my obligation to celebrate July 4th because of all the people who made significant sacrifices, including losing their lives to mobs and assassins so that I could be included in the "We" of "We the People." I proudly celebrate Juneteenth and July 4th as a reflection and celebration of my African and American heritages. It is important for elementary and early childhood educators to let students of all races know that it is important to learn about all of America's history.

Reflective Questions

I now invite you to reflect on the ideas presented in this chapter.

1. What is your next step in continuing to learn about the real history of the US?
2. What aspects of your social studies curriculum do you find problematic and why are they problematic? If you don't have a curriculum, examine what you are using/created. Consider the following sub-questions:
   a. Whose voices are most present and in what way are they presented?
   b. Whose stories are silenced, hardly mentioned, or mischaracterized?
   c. What events are not fully described, developed, or are written with biases?
   d. Who has written the histories you are telling (i.e., are white people narrating others' experiences and stories)? How is that perspective skewing the narrative and what are the ramifications of that limiting perspective?
   e. Are you only using tertiary courses? Could primary sources play a larger role in your teaching?
   f. What types of questions do you pose for students?

3. How do you routinely address civic education? How could it be increased to lead to civic engagement in the real world?
4. Do students see the connection between civic engagement and their roles as antiracists? How could you strengthen that connection?
5. What obstacles might you face when working to revise your social studies curricula and what might you try to overcome those barriers?
6. Imagine you are at an assembly and a student doesn't rise for the National Anthem. A teacher next to you starts to get very upset saying, "That's disrespectful. My father is a veteran and by not standing, that student is disrespecting my father and family's sacrifices." What do you do or say in response?

References

1619 Books (2023). The 1619 project. *Penguin Random House.* https://1619books.com/

Associated Press (2022, Oct. 31). The men exonerated in the Malcolm X killing will receive $36 million. *National Public Radio.* https://www.npr.org/2022/10/31/1132757141/the-men-exonerated-in-the-malcolm-x-killing-will-receive-36-million

Bartlett, K. (2015, Feb. 20). Why Malcolm X is getting written out of history. *Newsweek.* https://www.newsweek.com/2015/02/27/i-worry-my-father-being-written-out-history-307941.html

Behm, A., Fryar, C., Hunter, E., Leake, E., Lewis, S. L., & Miller-Davenport, S. (2020). Decolonizing history: Enquiry and practice. *History Workshop Journal, 89*, 169–191. https://doi.org/10.1093/hwj/dbz052

Bracken, K. Boyer, M., Fortin, J., Lieberman, & Throop, N. (2022, Aug. 17). What's actually being taught in history class. *New York Times.*

Coleman-Mortley, A. (2020, July 31). We need a civic education evolution to address racial injustice. *iCivics.* https://www.icivics.org/news/blog-post/we-need-civic-education-evolution-address-racial-injustice

Criss, D. (2019, Feb. 19). Here's why students don't have to recite the Pledge of Allegiance. *CNN.* https://www.cnn.com/2019/02/19/us/pledge-of-allegiance-explainer-trnd/index.html

Doyle, J., & Doyle, C. L. (2020, July 14). How should teachers handle the movement to 'rewrite' high school history? Embrace it. *Education Week.* https://www.edweek.org/teaching-learning/opinion-how-should-teachers-handle-the-movement-to-rewrite-high-school-history-embrace-it/2020/07

Erdman, C. (2021, Apr. 5). History in its entirety: How whitewashed history education leaves much of history, students out. *The Badger Herald.* https://badgerherald.com/features /2021/04/05/history-in-its-entirety-how-whitewashed-history-education-leave-much-of-history-students-out/

Kendi, I. X. (2017). *Stamped from the beginning: The definitive history of racist ideas in America.* Bold Type Books.

League of Women Voters of Delaware (n.d.). *What is civics?* https://my.lwv.org/delaware/government/what-civics

Loewen, J. (2018). *Lies my teacher told me: Everything your American history textbook got wrong.* The New Press.

Monticello.org (n.d.). *Thomas Jefferson and Sally Hemings.* https://www.monticello.org/thomas-jefferson/jefferson-slavery/thomas-jefferson-and-sally-hemings-a-brief-account/#:~:text=By%20Madison%20Hemings's%20and%20other,Jefferson%20(1748%2D1782)

National Center for Education Statistics (2023). Condition of Education: Concentration of public school students eligible for free or reduced-price lunch. *U.S. Department of Education, Institute of Education Sciences.* https://nces.ed.gov/programs/coe/indicator/clb.

National Council for the Social Studies (n.d.). College, career, and civic life (C3) *Framework for social studies state standards.* https://www.socialstudies.org/standards/c3

Stearns, P. N. (2020). Why study history? *American Historical Association.* https://www.historians.org/about-aha-and-membership/aha-history-and-archives/historical-archives/why-study-history-(1998)#:~:text=History%20Contributes%20to%20Moral%20Understanding&text=Studying%20the%20stories%20of%20individuals,have%20faced%20in%20difficult%20settings

Wiencek, H. (2012). The dark side of Thomas Jefferson. *Smithsonian Magazine.* https://www.smithsonianmag.com/history/the-dark-side-of-thomas-jefferson-35976004/

Will, M. (2023, Mar. 7). When it comes to social studies, elementary teachers are on their own. *Education Week*. https://www.edweek.org/teaching-learning/when-it-comes-to-social-studies-elementary-teachers-are-on-their-own/2023/03

Winthrop, R. (2020, June 4). The need for civic education in 21st-centruy schools. *Brookings*. https://www.brookings.edu/articles/the-need-for-civic-education-in-21st-century-schools/

9

Social-Emotional Learning Approaches

Racial Work *Is* Emotional Work

When I started working on being more aware of my privileges and the power that my whiteness held and the social capital I had, but didn't earn, it was like seeing something you can't unsee. I couldn't just learn about systemic racism and say, "wow, that really sucks for people who don't look like me" and move on with my life the same. The need to end systemic racism "bulldozed a road down the center of my mind" and I hope the same has happened, or is in the process of happening, for you by reading this book. Having something hit you that hard can be life-changing, motivating, and inspire you to enact real change. That's awesome! Embrace this initiated, activist version of yourself!

While this is all so inspiring and your engines are revved up for this work, it's okay to acknowledge how tiring and depleting it can be sometimes, too. I know that for myself, as a white woman, I didn't want to admit that it was hard work at first. I thought, since I never had to experience the oppression that Black, Indigenous, People of Color (BIPOC) have faced, due to my whiteness, I had no right to feel overwhelmed, frustrated, or any sort of negative emotions. While I don't face the daily racism that others face, I learned that it's okay to *have feelings* as I pursue my antiracist journey. Guilt, shame, anger, sadness are all part of the process. We can't act "fine" all the time if we are doing this work correctly because that's simply not healthy. Coming from experience, shedding tears and screaming into pillows are part of the process.

Let's face it. This work isn't meant to be a trip to Disney Land. When you think of a Friday night after work, how do you like to spend your time? At the end of a long workweek, we like to have fun and relax, right? So, for most people, a relaxing or fun activity isn't reading books about how to be antiracist or participating in a workshop or seminar on biases. Such activities aren't a Friday night activity because they aren't intended to be relaxing or fun. Rather, they are expected to be challenging and uncomfortable. For our own mental and emotional health, and for that of our students, we need to fully acknowledge and respect the taxing nature of becoming and being antiracist.

This chapter will address how to cope with our own emotions as we become antiracist and how to support our students' emotions. Self-care is an essential component explored. In addition, this chapter discusses how to build empathetic skills in white students when understanding experiences of people of other races and acknowledging the lack of understanding that inherently comes with this work because as white people, we will never truly understand what it is like to be a BIPOC person in America. Fostering a sense of our own white culture as an avenue for identity formation is essential and described as well. A useful framework to structure a Social-Emotional Learning (SEL) approach is through the Collaborative for Academic, Social, and Emotional Learning (CASEL) Framework, which will be examined within this context of antiracist development.

Emotional Support for Ourselves and Each Other

In Chapter 5, we discussed the parameters of having safe and brave conversations in our classrooms with students, utilizing student-generated parameters as a basis. However thorough you are in making expectations clear, there is no way to keep emotions out of antiracism work. In fact, trying to become antiracist devoid of expressing emotions means that you're not engaging authentically in the work. Becoming antiracist involves deep, personal change; it means uprooting ideas and norms that are most familiar to you and turning them upside down and inside out. It involves a level of vulnerability that, if done correctly, should make your skin crawl at times. As unappetizing as it sounds, that's how it should feel at times. That's not to say that becoming an antiracist doesn't bring moments of joy, bonding, curiosity, and excitement. Those desirable qualities just don't come without the negative emotions.

Antiracism work can feel like an emotional rollercoaster. One day I'm deep in a book about critical race pedagogies and feeling inspired to shift some of my lessons using new strategies to engage student voice more regarding modern racial issues, the next day I'm in tears after class because a student calls me out on a microaggression I had no idea I committed. No wonder I go to bed tired every night! It's important for you and your students, and anyone starting their antiracist journeys, that the whole range of emotions is part of it. It is essential, however, to recognize that there is a time and a place to feel certain emotions.

As a scholar in antiracist education, I make lots of mistakes, and I invite others to call me in or call me out (DiAngelo, 2018) when that occurs. Depending on what my error was dictates my emotional response. Sometimes, it's using the wrong term and I might not be careful about my word choice. Other times, I say or do something that may have made another person feel bad in some way. Those situations hit me in the gut. When I cause someone else to elicit a negative emotion, it makes me feel utterly terrible. I've learned through countless resources and through friends of color, that it is best to apologize, recognize the wrongdoing, validate the other person's response, and move on (Williams, 2020). Before learning that, I used to get overly defensive. Then, I started reading how wrong it was to get defensive and wanted to work on that response. But, I then started to go too far the other direction. I would opt to apologize, apologize some more, and then, if possible, apologize even more. What I didn't realize was that approach of apologizing *ad nauseum* actually makes BIPOC feel even worse about the situation. Suddenly, not only do they feel hurt by the microaggression that you have committed, but now they see how much you're groveling and overreacting that they regret even having the courage to approach you about it. Profuse apology makes it more about you than about them. Just another example of whiteness needing to be the center of attention and sympathy.

Self-Care for White Antiracists
Let's now unpack some recommendations made for white people dedicated to antiracism work. These recommendations are first positioned for you, as an adult, but then we consider how they could also work for our students, too.

Recommendation 1: Self-Care Isn't an Excuse
The first recommendation is to not use self-care as an excuse to not commit yourself to being an antiracist (Borges, 2020). Just because it's hard doesn't mean that as white people it is okay to say, "I need to take care of myself, and this is too much for me." The very notion that white people even have the option to tune out speaks to the white supremacy that makes race an idea that white people don't *need* to think about routinely. It's important to remember that learning about racism and our biases is hard and challenging; however, it is *not* ruining our mental health. Borges (2020) emphasizes there's a major difference between something that is *hard* and something that is *damaging* our mental health, and antiracism is just *hard*. When working with our students, I advise being transparent about the struggles you face in becoming antiracist and modeling that it's challenging for you, but you understand you must keep going. I also see value in sharing that "rocking our own boats" may feel difficult, but "rocking the boats" that hold our loved ones can feel even harder, but matters greatly (Nolan, 2022). This can't be solitary work, which is why you, as the teacher, are bringing this work to some of the most important people in your life: your students. In essence, white people worked together to create white supremacy, and they need to work together to dismantle it, too (not to say the BIPOC

involvement isn't integral, though). As Nolan (2022) describes, "A white person who 'does the work' in isolation is like a pianist playing in a sealed room." They can hear their own music, feel transformed personally, but they shouldn't expect the world to be dancing and feeling the same. We need to, and we need our students to, share the music.

Recommendation 2: Avoid Media Overload

A second recommendation is to control your media consumption (Borges, 2020). Yes, as teachers and antiracist humans, we need to stay current on the news. However, there are limits. Do you find yourself mindlessly scrolling and feeling drained by stories of racism, inequity, and conflict and end up wanting to throw your phone across the room out of frustration with the world? Oh, the dreaded "doomscrolling." Yup, I've been there. Feelings of despair, doubt, and defeat have hit me numerous times, even while researching for this very book! Borges (2020) reminds us that constantly consuming media can drain us from doing what matters: taking action. In fact, doomscrolling "prevents you from paying attention to your thoughts and feelings" and means that you aren't considering how detrimental the media is on you (Deering, 2023). Setting boundaries as to when you'll shut off from scrolling is helpful. If you're up for a challenge, you might even consider making a rule with yourself that for every hour spent scrolling, you must think about one action you are going to take to support a cause you're boosting or sharing. One final note regarding social media is that feuds in the comments section go nowhere and only can make you upset. Use that time and energy in more effective ways in your community because no Instagram comment is going to change a strangers' perspective and outlook on the world. This is an awesome reminder to share with our older elementary students who are likely already on social media.

Recommendation 3: Remember That This Is a Marathon, Not a Sprint

The third recommendation is to think about being antiracist as a lifelong marathon, not a sprint with a clear endpoint

(Borges, 2020). This means that as white antiracists, we need stamina. Critically reflect routinely as to why you are doing this work. Remind yourself that you're not doing this just because it's a topic of focus in the news and on social media, because when the buzz fades (which some argue it largely has faded a couple of years after the racial reckoning of the summer of 2020), you'll still be doing the work. I've had many people in my life post to social media how much they care about antiracism by resharing inspiring quotes and selfies at Black Lives Matter rallies, planning events to show racial solidarity, and purchasing items from black-owned businesses the months following the summer of 2020. That was the "cool" thing to do at the time and if you were a white person *not* doing those things, you felt like you risked being called a racist and people may make political assumptions about you. Some have even said that white people gentrified the Black Lives Matter movement in the summer of 2020 (Logan, 2020). In simple terms, many white people were showing up for themselves, not the cause. They shifted the focus from who rallies were *really* about: black people. Logan (2020) writes that the numbers show how white people cared when racial justice was all over the news, but their attention and compassion weren't authentic or strong enough to last. She adds, "according to a June [2020] poll, 45% of white people surveyed found racism to be a 'big problem.' And by the time her September 2020 article was published, that number had fallen to 38%" (Logan, 2020). We also saw loads of major and local businesses release public statements against racism. But what are these individuals and organizations doing today? Did they follow through on promises and remain dedicated to the work? Is antiracism as much of a priority to them as they made it sound back in the wake of the summer of 2020? I think that everyone needs a reminder as to why we should care and why this work matters. Consistent encouragement to remember to hold each other accountable to this work, especially if you're publicly making statements about it, matters monumentally. I think it's worthwhile to provide students opportunities to uncover *why* they should be antiracist and for you to share *your* reasons. Again, this requires vulnerability, but such modeling is pivotal for inspiring your students' trajectories.

Recommendation 4: Developing a Sense of Your Own White Identity and Culture

A fourth recommendation to consider is recognizing that our white racial identity is on a continuum and reflecting where you land on it to consider steps toward eventual autonomy. Helms (1995) provides a framework that covers the following stages: (1) Contact: Ethnic and racial differences carry little weight to a person and colorblindness is the prevailing perspective. (2) Disintegration: The person's idea of "colorblindness" is challenged, and the person begins to recognize privileges that come with their whiteness. (3) Reintegration: This is when a person's guilt and shame lead to thoughts like, "white people must have privileges because they deserve them" and foster an attitude of "blame-the-victim." (4) Pseudo-Independence: This stage is achieved if the person can ward off the feelings described in Reintegration. In this stage, they start making progress on their own white racial identity but turn to BIPOC to confront and address racism, not themselves. Being white and anti-racist are not hand-in-hand yet. (5) Immersion/Emerson: Being white and antiracist finally go together. The person develops an understanding of BIPOC experiences and works to connect with other white people to work on racial injustice. (6) Autonomy: The person views their whiteness positively, which is part of their ability to work toward antiracism.

An idea that truly struck a chord with me in this process of white racial identity is considering a positive view of ourselves as white people. When I have thought of someone being proud of their whiteness, my mind has gone to think about white supremacists. However, understanding what makes us who we are as white people can be truly helpful in not only mitigating feeling guilty over being white but can inspire antiracist actions (Tochluk & Saxman, 2023). Positive white racial identity can lead to taking steps toward authentic antiracism as part of our identities. I have been personally trying to consider what qualities of my white culture provide me a sense of belonging to a group that is motivated to see widespread social justice. For example, my home culture is one rooted in consistent reflections on what we are thankful for (we share these with each other nightly). That's part of our culture and I'm proud of that personally, as well as how such a cultural aspect provides me opportunities to consider how I can work toward being thankful for opportunities to support antiracism. I feel like I had developed an understanding either that white culture didn't exist or that anyone who embraces white culture must be holding onto aspects of society that center whiteness and white privilege. I've come to realize that white people have a culture, and it doesn't need to be one rooted in such negativity. I can be proud of my home values, recipes passed down in my lineage, and traditions we hold dear. I have culture, and it's okay for me to be proud of it. At the end of this chapter, I encourage you to reflect upon your culture as white person and how aspects of it make you personally proud and can also be tools toward change.

Avoiding Burnout and Maintaining Motivation

Avoiding burnout is a major part of maintaining stamina. Actions to give back and contribute to ending systemic racism that motivate you and energize you mixed with ones that leave you feeling drained are important to feel balanced. Borges (2020) gives the example that if you're not a very social person and get drained from being around lots of people, then maybe going to protests and large events all the time isn't the best fit for you. Consider other avenues that feel more sustainable, like starting a book club, or volunteering to help plan a Juneteenth event. Tatiana Mac (n.d.) provides a helpful list of "sustainable strategies for activism" to help white people show up single every day. Mac (n.d.) suggests white people consider the following:

1. If you are asking a lot of questions and receiving a plethora of answers and feel overwhelmed, consider making a list and take time to read a variety of sources about a single topic.
2. Consider not making just one big donation to a social justice cause all at once. Rather, consider making recurring donations that are within your budget (and time donations work this way, too. Not just monetary donations).
3. If you're trying to be a part of many book clubs and feel overloaded to be prepared to discuss, try incorporating

black authors into your everyday reading (whether they are books about race or simply pleasure reading). This goes for what we watch as well, so consider more black-produced films and shows.
4. Evaluate who you're supporting when you make purchases. While certain retailers are popular due to convenience and money-saving deals, could you shift some routine purchases to black-owned businesses?
5. Make a plan when the work feels lonely. As a white person, I was focused and dedicated to antiracism before the summer of 2020. Then, suddenly, I felt like I had such a community of white folks joining me. Now, as I write this book, many of those white folks have disregarded the movement. Build connections with people who are like-minded to you and are dedicated for the long haul to hold each other accountable and feel motivated.
6. You're not cramming for a test, so no need to rush the learning process. Take the time to digest, reflect, and critically examine new ideas you learn.
7. Purposefully and thoughtfully extend your energies. As previously mentioned, "social media trolls" are not worth your time. Rather, have deep conversations with loved ones and those who can help make change, like colleagues and leaders.
8. Consider your democratic role in ending systemic racism. This means learning about politicians for whom you vote, policies and legislation that need revision, and more. Be an informed citizen to enact change.
9. Consider your criteria for participation in something. Does the event or organization that is asking for your involvement match your ideas and expectations for raising/supporting black voices? If not, how will you respond and possibly decline?

Motivation Through Real-Life Experiences and Service
I have found my own motivation comes largely through the impact I can have in the real world. Raising BIPOC voices at work and in my community, actively listening to BIPOC

voices in meetings and forums, and supporting BIPOC-owned businesses are just a few small actions that can clearly show me that I can have an impact on racial equity. For instance, encouraging a BIPOC colleague's voice at a meeting and seeing their ideas enacted provides that instant fuel for me to power through those days when I feel I have very little impact. With an issue as daunting as racial equity teasing me constantly like it's too big for me to address, I reflect on those moments where I helped others succeed. Sometimes we all need to see the small impacts we have to know that a larger impact is possible. Our students may not be convinced that they can have an impact until they try it out in the real world. I also stay motivated when I witness my students feeling ignited to create change in the real world, thanks to their increased motivation.

In my experience as a classroom teacher, I have seen student engagement skyrocket when children feel like they are learning through "doing" in the real world. Having students self-reflect on how they'd like to help by providing them with starter ideas may lead to a class project or volunteerism. Service-learning has the potential to be valuable, but it is integral to not fall into the white-savior approach to helping others. As Mitchell et al. (2012) found that most service-learning occurs when white college students volunteer in low-income, more racially diverse places. These experiences have lacked three elements that could make these experiences more authentic learning opportunities to lead to systemic change, rather than prompting white saviorism. These "non-whitecentric" approaches are to (1) teachers check their own assumptions about their students, the community, and the goals of the service-learning experience, (2) frame service-learning in a way that promotes critical examination of racism and systemic oppression, and (3) lead discussions explicitly on race before, during, and after the service-learning project.

When picking or considering service-learning opportunities, involve students in reflecting on their skill sets that they bring to the table. With older students, you may want to have them practice self-reflecting on their personalities, strengths, and areas of growth when considering what ways they can help with a local issue. Asset mapping is a strategy where students make a web of their experiences and the skills and traits that depict who they are as students and people in a more general sense. I have done this with college students to help with group projects and can see this working well for upper elementary students before group projects or service-learning endeavors (Stoddard & Pfeifer, 2020). Students could look at how their assets can extend beyond community-based projects and have the potential to aid in their activist roles in society to help end racial inequity in the US. I recommend modeling for students what strengths of your own help you contribute to the cause and what choices you make in response to your assets.

For early elementary students, doing a food drive and discussing food insecurity could be a useful gateway for discussing inequity. Every student can have a role and can be asked to think about what makes them good at that role. For example, maybe one student loves to draw and that skill helps them make the posters to hang around school to encourage non-perishable donations. Students are then practicing taking stock of their skill sets and seeing how they can aid a greater cause.

As you continue through this book, read other books, explore other sources, and more, refer back to this section and the included self-care list if you ever question your willpower to keep on the path of antiracism. When the marathon is feeling too much, remember that there are educators just like yourself struggling in the same ways. Find your network and utilize each other.

You'll Never Fully Understand, But Empathy Is Possible

This section explores how we, as white people, can have empathy toward BIPOC but not to the extent that BIPOC can have empathy toward each other. By definition, "empathy" is, "the action of understanding, being aware of, being sensitive to, and vicariously experiencing the feelings, thoughts, and experience of another" (Merriam-Webster, n.d.). Empathy is essential for teachers in cultivating culturally responsive pedagogy (Warren, 2018) and it is a necessary skill for all students. As white people, we are limited in the amount of empathy we can have because we will never know how it feels to be a BIPOC person in the US. We can imagine and try to relate experiences we have had that felt unfair or that a bias played against us. However, our white skin means that we have never faced systemic racism within the US. When considering this, I have been careful to respond to BIPOC friends when they share experiences of racism with phrases like, "I can only imagine how challenging that must have been" instead of, "I know exactly what you mean" or "I felt that way when this one time…" Trying to share a white experience of injustice to relate to a BIPOC's experience with racial injustice can belittle the racism that the person experienced and can feel like a microaggression to BIPOC.

As we dig into the idea of having students cultivate empathy for those outside of their own race, it is important to recognize other limitations of empathy. People tend to identify with individuals, not the collective, which can be exclusionary (Demby et al., 2020). When exploring and expressing empathy, we can't dissociate from ourselves and our subjectivity, so our biases can affect how we develop empathy. Similar to how we've unpacked being wary of stereotypes, we need to be careful to ensure that connecting with a single person's experience is not generating the notion in our minds that one person's experiences are representative of all BIPOC. Empathy, through a racial lens especially, requires astute self-awareness. As previously explored, self-awareness of our flaws, biases, and how our perspectives can be skewed, can help for a clearer view of others' experiences because we can do our best to "course correct" our viewpoints if we are aware of our perspectives' imperfections.

Why Empathy Matters and How It Manifests

So why does empathy matter in our students starting at a young age? Students need more than just academic knowledge and skill sets as contributing citizens and in the workplace one day. They need to know how to navigate the social complexities of the world and notice and work toward dismantling the systemic injustices that prevent society from functioning with respect and compassion (Manning, 2020). Empathy has the power to "open up students to deeper learning, drive clarity of thinking, and inspire engagement with the world—in other words, provide the emotional sustenance for outstanding human performance" (Markham, 2016). Empathy is part of collaborations and is associated with positive emotions like appreciation, feeling open, and curiosity. Furthermore, from a biological and psychological standpoint, empathy ignites the frontal lobe of the brain. This is the part of the brain that is responsible for planning, execution, creativity, and problem-solving—all essential for optimal learning, also known as the "flow state." Why would empathy *not* be emphasized in schools if it can optimize student learning and performance? Seems a tad counterintuitive to me. Yet, we live in a test-centric, academically stringent society that views empathy-building as a "soft skill" that can be tacked on if there's time. However, empathy is a 21st-century skill that is necessary for societal unity. Empathy could be considered the key to effective equity-based reforms targeting systemic oppression (El Mallah & Pfister, 2022).

I agree with proponents that argue that empathy could be the key to dismantling white racism (Lanzoni, 2019). Throughout US history, there have been numerous white politicians claiming to be genuine promoters of racial equity but couldn't fully commit themselves due to political interests. As James Baldwin, a civil rights activist and writer, rationalized this, those politicians did not see Black Americans as "another man like himself." In short, those white politicians were unable to see shared humanity (i.e., we are all human) and mutual respect. This boils down to a lack of empathy. Any notion of white superiority inhibits interracial empathy (Lanzoni, 2019). Kenneth Clark, a NY psychologist and former Howard University Trustee, was long committed to research pertaining to the psychology of race. His collection of social science data that correlated segregated schools with black students' psychological distress played an integral role in desegregating public schools in *Brown v. Board.* Clark contended that when people connect with those who are similar to ourselves is "parochial empathy," which is not the full extent of empathy. Clark thought that *real* empathy asks white people to "transcend the barriers of their own minds" by listening to what their hearts told them. He saw a type of empathy that focuses on shared humanity. Since empathy relies on at least one point of relatability, which for white people practicing empathy for BIPOC, humanity is a starting point for seeing the world through someone else's eyes.

When viewing and learning of other people's experiences, we either imagine those experiences happening to ourselves by seeing shared qualities (like humanity, age, gender, etc.) or we can focus on the differences between ourselves and the person we are viewing or learning about and block an empathic response (Segal, 2021). In fact, research has shown, through a deep dive into neural responses, that people learn to see other races in ways that block empathic responses. As sad as that may sound, it means that we can learn to develop empathic tendencies toward other races, too. However, like learning a language, the older we get, the harder this process is. Use this as an emphasis that developing empathy in children is more important than ever if we yearn for systemic change. There are two branches of empathy: interpersonal and social. Interpersonal empathy is built through interacting with others. Social empathy builds off interpersonal empathy and connects to historical events and larger social systems and how they affect people who are different than you (Segal, 2021). George Floyd's death sparking people to join the BLM Movement was an example of people responding with interpersonal empathy. The decline in BLM support as time went on, however, shows a lack of mass social empathy. In sum, it is challenging to have people see structural racism. It's easier to look at one person's death at the hands of police to feel activated, but social empathy requires a deep dive into the circumstances of his death and the history and conditions that contributed to his death.

So, if you're in a learning environment with only white people, it is challenging to have students authentically develop interpersonal empathy. How can you build relationships with people of different races when everyone around you is the same race as you? If simply watching George Floyd's death online could evoke interpersonal empathy, it is possible to develop interpersonal empathy without actually interacting directly with another person. The caveat here is that since relationship-building is unequivocally important, these suggestions are no replacement for building authentic relationships with people. As white teachers, we need to acknowledge that our students, by attending predominantly white schools, will lack the interracial empathy that students in diverse schools will have. So as people like to say that predominantly white schools "have more to offer their students than diverse schools" because of funding and resources, a huge "offering" that white schools lack, is interracial relationships, and that's arguably, more important than all the instructional technology and field trips in the world. So, take this as yet another reminder that racial integration of our schools is the *real answer*.

Practical Approaches to Evoking Racial Empathy

For many of us white folks who grew up segregated, developing empathy for people of other races doesn't happen until college or the workplace, when we first get to know BIPOC. I know that was the case for me. I went off to college and had never spent so much time with so many people of different races, ethnicities, sexual orientations, gender identities, religions, and more. This was my first prolonged experience being around BIPOC—long enough to form relationships. Prior to that, I had no experiences at school that were meant to promote my interpersonal empathy for BIPOC. Building these skills requires reflection and intention, so while maybe I read a book about a black character experiencing racism, I wasn't given the tools to explore that through an empathic lens. With the understanding that white teachers supporting white classes in developing interpersonal empathy for BIPOC needs to happen without the most important element (BIPOC in the room), we can explore strategies for working with students to develop these skills as much as possible so that white students are at least a step closer to developing social empathy by the time they go to college or enter the workplace.

Strategy 1: Pen-Pals

While not physically present, students can still get to know and feel connected to students the same age as them through becoming pen-pals. This is like the book *Same, Same, But Different*. Students get to explore aspects of themselves and their lives that are similar and unpack their differences. Pen-pals can be a great way to get students to connect with peers who are of the same age, giving a nice baseline commonality (other than humanity), which we know is important when developing empathy, as previously discussed. There are a variety of sites that allow teachers to connect and set up writing partnerships (Bizzarri, 2020). These writing relationships can lead to purposeful conversations with your students about what they are learning and to consider the larger contexts that have affected how different their lives are from their pen-pals.

Strategy 2: Books
Reading first-person narratives and diaries can help students consider the perspectives of BIPOC from modern-day or historically. When considering if a book truly evokes empathy, it's important to question if it challenges students to understand the characters who are and are not like them. Children's books that can balance a particular set of elements, that Kucirkova (2019) promotes in their article, are useful for teacher consideration. Kucirkova (2019) encourages having books that (1) have cognitive and affective empathy. This means that the story not only prompts students to practice taking another's perspective but also ignites an emotional response to the character's experiences. (2) The book encourages students to identify who is "in group or out group," which means delineating who is like them and who is unlike them. (3) The story feels immersive, like the reader is actually there, making the experience feel more real. (4) The story employs a narrative style that promotes empathy. Specific narrative style could mean considering a particular branch of fiction or nonfiction that feels more realistic to students, for example. The format of the story could also play a role, like how oral storytelling can be more affective at promoting empathy than writing does. (5) Adults mediating the empathic experience is essential, through scaffolded discussions and reflective questions. Such questions can help students not fall into sympathy or a sense of pity for people

different from them, as sympathy lacks the action element (Livingston, 2020). Empathy leads to getting students to ask, "Okay, now that you know this is how some people experience things, do you care enough to do something about it?" That action-oriented caring can lead to solidarity and social justice, not just white folks feeling bad for BIPOC. Feeling bad for someone else with no actions contributes nothing toward change.

Strategy 3: Exposure and Education

Hearing BIPOC tell their perspectives in a brave, safe space, with raw emotion, their own natural vocal fluctuations and cadence, and facial expressions have the power to evoke visceral reactions in students. Watching and listening to a person recount something that happened to them can feel immersive and can lead to students feeling a sense of empathy for the speaker. Video interviews and guest speakers can be hugely influential on our students in what can be called "psychologically safe listening sessions" (Livingston, 2020). Exposure to BIPOC's lived experiences then can lead to explicit education opportunities, like showing the systemic conditions that make that one person's experiences not solitary. The larger context can then lead to conversations about actions to make widespread change.

Social-Emotional Learning through an Antiracist Lens

SEL curricula in schools can vary greatly. I recall implementing a program as a student-teacher in first grade and as a fifth-grade teacher in which I would have a picture of a scene on a large card that I would show students. I would narrate the scenario and then ask the students questions to reflect upon and consider how they would respond in that situation. It wasn't until writing this book that I realized how racially blind the curriculum was. There were no instances where racism or biases played a role or even any character descriptions that explored the characters' racial identities and how they varied.

Caven (2020) explains that when SEL curricula don't acknowledge students' race and cultures, it means that they are only reflecting the white-centered cultural norms and don't even recognize what white culture is. Not identifying, embracing, and exploring racial and cultural factors means that the curriculum implies students' diverse backgrounds are deficits. When SEL curricula do not address the systemic oppression of which BIPOC students are subjected, these curricula risk implying that "the social and emotional challenges that students do encounter are the result of individual shortcomings, rather than the byproduct of oppression" (Caven, 2020). These curricula warrant serious revision.

Let's explore how SEL curricula can be antiracist and help all students build empathy and reflect on society in a more accurate way. An antiracist SEL curriculum would place value and recognition that students with different backgrounds and experiences will have developed different social and emotional skills. White students who have largely only socialized with other white people likely have little experience or knowledge of other races' cultures. For example, white students may not understand that African American vernacular is a dialect of English and to be respectful of it, rather than carrying forward the white supremacist falsehood that such language indicates a lack of education. The CASEL framework provides a baseline for exploring antiracist SEL in predominantly white learning environments next.

CASEL Framework

The CASEL framework for SEL is designed to promote SEL skills in four settings: classrooms, entire schools, at home with families and caregivers, and in the larger community (CASEL, 2023). Their pervasive, well-rounded approach communicates to students that SEL is a life skill, not just one to be used on occasion. The CASEL framework addresses five competencies: self-awareness, self-management, social awareness, relationship skills, and responsible decision-making. Each of these interrelated areas has the potential to play an important role in students becoming antiracist. Let's explore each of these five competencies to see how they can tie into antiracism in our students.

Self-Awareness

Have you noticed a theme in this book that self-reflection is essential in addressing biases and being an antiracist? We've talked about self-awareness to understand how the things we do and say could be considered microaggressions and how self-awareness of our biases can help us address them. As Kendi states, "being an antiracist requires persistent self-awareness, constant self-criticism, and regular self-examination" (Taylor, 2019). A sense of self encompasses a communal identity that can be rooted in a shared race or culture. As discussed earlier, it is important for white students to understand their whiteness and the societal implications of it. White students can learn that they share an ethnic-racial identity (ERI) with each other in your classroom and can use that network to gain clarity about the role that their shared race has in their lives. "A healthy sense of ERI is important for psychological, academic, and social well-being" (Jagers et al., 2018, p. 5). In essence, white students can see their shared whiteness as an asset in supporting each other to redefine what it means to be a white person in America and not repeat history. Like discussed earlier, students can go through negative emotions about their whiteness, but the lasting sentiment should be one of motivation for the future. When the cultural norms have promoted a message that white people are entitled and dominant, a focus on self-awareness can help replace these messages with ones that communicate the truth about whiteness in society and what it can be. Positive connotations through white cultural exploration can be useful, too (Tochlick & Saxon, 2023).

Self-Management

Self-management refers to self-regulation of emotions, management of stress, self-control, self-motivation, and working toward goals (Jagers et al., 2018). All of these components of self-management connect to becoming antiracist. First, regarding emotional self-regulation, it's no secret that this work is inherently emotional. It can be challenging to be called out (or called in) for something we say or do and not have an emotional response. We've discussed avoiding overly apologizing in response to BIPOC, for example. We've also talked about how it can be challenging to not feel sad, guilty, and a sense of pity for BIPOC all the time, but how important it is to maintain positivity for the future. Second, for stress management, much of this chapter discussed self-care when on the lifelong antiracism journey to avoid burnout and to be actively involved for the long haul. Third, regarding self-control and self-motivation, we have control in working on our biases and how we participate in society. Everyone has a choice: either contribute to perpetuating inequitable norms and systemic oppression or do your part to disrupt them. While the issues can feel too large to bear, every student has the power to be a change-maker, which is reliant on their self-control and self-motivation. Finally, when developing self-management, it's important for students to set goals and practice working toward those goals. Goals around addressing biases can be a fantastic way to incorporate antiracism in students' SEL.

Social Awareness
Social awareness is being able to develop empathy, respect diversity, recognize social and ethical behavioral norms, and understand supports at home, at school, and in the community (Jagers et al., 2018). Remember when we explored the idea of having our white students openly view and discuss educational inequities between predominantly white schools and predominantly BIPOC schools? That activity was a step toward students recognizing society privileging white students over BIPOC students. An important part of social awareness is when students can notice when, and in what ways, society is choosing different identity categories to privilege (race, gender affiliation, sexual orientation, language, etc.). Noticing systemic biases is a skill set that can help students consider their roles in addressing inequities on a societal scale. Social awareness also can get students to think about how their white privilege plays a role in disadvantaging others and to consider what they can do about it.

Relationship Skills
Relationship skills refer to connecting with a diverse array of people (individually and in groups), asking for help when needed, and communication, cooperation, and conflict-resolution skills

(Jagers et al., 2018). If a student is struggling with self-awareness, self-management, and/or social awareness, chances are, they will struggle with relationship-building. Students in predominantly white schools lack opportunities to practice establishing and maintaining relationships with peers and adults that are of different races when compared to students who attend more diverse schools. People of different races and backgrounds have varying social cues and when white students have never been exposed to those differences, it can cause them to misinterpret the BIPOC person and the relationship could become strained, and conflict can even arise. This is one tenet of the CASEL framework that is challenging for classroom teachers to implement authentically through an antiracist lens since there aren't BIPOC students in the classroom or school with whom students can build relationships. School recruitment to diversify the student body is an important step toward racial integration but since that's a long-term solution, in the meantime, parental and community support needs to come into play. Parents and caregivers can work on having their children do extracurricular activities in a more diverse city/town, for example. However, please note that racially diverse settings for extracurriculars are still extremely limiting and cannot fully make up for the amount of interracial relationship-building children could get during the school day at a racially diverse school. Relationship-building happens through experience. We can teach our white students how to interact with BIPOC peers "until the cows come home," but it's not until white students get the chance to interact with BIPOC peers, make mistakes, and try again, that they will truly learn and develop this skill.

Responsible Decision-Making
Responsible decision-making skills connote students considering their responsibility to maintain the well-being of others and to behave ethically themselves. In addition, students think about the consequences for their actions and make choices that support the well-being of themselves, their relationships, and their school (Jagers et al., 2018). Policies and regulations are in response to leaders and groups making decisions. Those decision-makers can

establish systems that are inequitable. Our students are future voters and leaders who have the power to influence the systems in place. Their decisions can affect the systemic inequities that our society faces today. "Nurturing students' understanding of systemic or structural explanations for differential treatment and outcomes, together with relationship skills..." can be done in diverse or mono-racial settings (Jagers et al., 2018, pp. 7–8). Our students benefit from exercises, activities, and opportunities focused on making decisions that lead to structures that are equitable and supportive to people of all backgrounds.

As we work on supporting our students' SEL, don't forget that adult SEL matters, too. We, as teachers, can further develop our SEL skills, especially through an antiracist lens. Making antiracist SEL a school cultural norm and encouraging parents and caregivers to carry these messages and opportunities to practice together at home can then help shift the community toward one where equity is a priority. While this book may have uncovered areas of history you need to explore and biases you never knew you had, let this be yet another call to action to spend some time committing yourself to social-emotional learning as well.

Dr. McGowan Weighs In

It is important for white teachers involved in antiracist teaching to tend to their own social-emotional well-being as they support the social-emotional well-being of their white students. According to Daniel Goleman, the adult version of social-emotional development is emotional intelligence. Goleman identifies five components associated with emotional intelligence: self-awareness, self-regulation, self-management, social awareness, and relationship management. The CASEL framework addresses five competencies for children: self-awareness, self-management, social awareness, relationship skills, and responsible decision-making. We can see the connections between the CASEL framework focused on children's social-emotional development and Goleman's theory of emotional intelligence focused on teachers' social-emotional development. Reflection, flexibility, and empathy are prominently featured in the CASEL framework and emotional intelligence. Social-emotional development and emotional intelligence are the foundations for all of the other antiracist-focused content areas.

Reflective Questions

I now invite you to reflect on the ideas presented in this chapter.

1. What is a time that you were called out for a microaggression? Describe the emotional journey you were on and how you responded to the person. What would you do differently next time?
2. Which of Mac's "sustainable strategies for activism" struck a chord with you and why?
3. What are your next steps to practicing self-care so that you remain committed to being antiracist for the long haul?
4. How would you describe your own "white culture"? What aspects can also be used to leverage antiracism?
5. How do you motivate students to be involved in service learning while concurrently avoiding white saviorism? If you don't do service learning, what are some ways you could do so while avoiding white saviorism?
6. How have you evoked empathy in your students previously? What are your plans to have students explore empathy with a racial focus, without having students land on sympathy?
7. Consider the social-emotional curricula and/or materials that you have been using. How do they align with the CASEL framework through a racial lens? How could you modify it to better address antiracism?
8. When reviewing the five tenets of SEL in the CASEL framework, what are one or two tenets you feel you need to practice more? What are your next steps to practice and improve?

References

Bizzarri, A. (2020, Mar. 23). Virtual pen pals: 5 resources for connecting kids around the world. *We are Teachers*. https://www.weareteachers.com/virtual-pen-pals/

Borges, A. (2020, June 10). White people, we need to talk about 'self-care.' *Self*. https://www.self.com/story/white-people-self-care

Caven, M. (2020, July 27). Why we need an anti-racist approach to social and emotional learning. *Education Development Center*. https://www.edc.org/blog/why-we-need-anti-racist-approach-social-and-emotional-learning

Collaborative for Academic, Social, and Emotional Learning (2023). *What is the CASEL framework?*. https://casel.org/fundamentals-of-sel/what-is-the-casel-framework/

Deering, S. (2023, May 19). How 'doomscrolling' impacts your mental health—and how to stop. *Very Well Mind*. https://www.verywellmind.com/what-is-doomscrolling-5088882

Demby, G., Escobar, N., & Kramer, S. K. (2020, Mar. 11). The limits of empathy. *NPR*. https://www.npr.org/2020/03/06/812864654/the-limits-of-empathy

DiAngelo, R. J. (2018). *White fragility: Why it's so hard for white people to talk about racism*. Beacon Press.

El Mallah, S. & Pfister, T. (2022, Feb. 1). Empathy as a tool for equity. *The Association for Supervision and Curriculum Development*. https://www.ascd.org/el/articles/empathy-as-a-tool-for-equity

Helms, J. E. (1995). An update of Helms's white and people of color racial identity models. In J. G. Ponterotto, J. M. Casa, L. S. Suzuki, & C. M. Alexander (Eds.), *Handbook of multicultural counseling* (pp. 181–198). Thousand Oaks, CA: Sage Publications.

Jagers, R. J., Rivas-Drake, D., & Borowski, T. (2018, Nov.). Equity and social and emotional learning: A cultural analysis. *Measuring SEL Using data to Inspire Practice*. https://drc.casel.org/uploads/sites/3/2019/02/Equity-Social-and-Emotional-Learning-A-Cultural-Analysis.pdf

Kucirkova, N. (2019). How could children's storybooks promote empathy? A conceptual framework based on developmental psychology and literary theory. *Frontiers in Psychology*, *10*, 121. https://doi.org/10.3389/fpsyg.2019.00121

Lanzoni, S. (2019, Feb. 22). Why empathy is the key to dismantling white racism. *The Washington Post.* https://www.washingtonpost.com/outlook/2019/02/22/why-empathy-is-key-dismantling-white-racism/

Livingston, R. (2020, Sept.–Oct.). How to promote racial equity in the workplace. *Harvard Business Review.* https://hbr.org/2020/09/how-to-promote-racial-equity-in-the-workplace

Logan, E. B. (2020, Sept. 8). White people have gentrified Black Lives Matter: It's a problem. *Los Angeles Times.* https://www.latimes.com/opinion/story/2020-09-04/black-lives-matter-white-people-portland-protests-nfl

Mac, T. (n.d.). Beware of burnout: Sustainable strategies for activism. https://www.tatianamac.com/posts/beware-of-burnout

Manning, N. (2020, June 26). Prioritizing empathy and anti-racism in schools. *PBS.* https://www.pbs.org/education/blog/prioritizing-empathy-and-anti-racism-in-schools

Markham, T. (2016, Nov. 16). Why empathy holds the key to transforming 21st century learning. *KQED.* https://www.kqed.org/mindshift/46980/why-empathy-holds-the-key-to-transforming-21st-century-learning

Merriam-Webster. (n.d.). *Empathy.* Merriam-Webster.com dictionary. https://www.merriam-webster.com/dictionary/empathy

Mitchell, T., Donahue, D., & Young-Law, C. (2012). Service learning as a pedagogy of whiteness. *Equity & Excellence in Education, 45*(4), 612–629. https://doi.org/10.1080/10665684.2012.715534

Nolan, S. (2022, Feb. 7). It's time for white people to have tough conversations with their white friends and relatives. *Time Magazine.* https://time.com/6145211/white-people-tough-conversations-race/

Segal, E. A. (2021, May 31). Does racism mean there's a lack of empathy? *Psychology Today.* https://www.psychologytoday.com/us/blog/social-empathy/202105/does-racism-mean-theres-lack-empathy

Stoddard, E., & Pfeifer, G. (2020). *Diversity, equity, and inclusion tools for teamwork: Asset mapping and team processing handbook.* https://digital.wpi.edu/concern/generic_works/8w32r8712?locale=en

Taylor, E. (2019, Aug. 15). Ibram X. Kendi says no one is 'not racist.' So what should we do? *NPR.* https://www.npr.org/2019/08/15/751070344/theres-no-such-thing-as-not-racist-in-ibram-x-kendis-how-to-be-an-anitracist

Tochluk, S., & Saxman, C. (2023). *Being white today: A roadmap for a positive antiracist life.* Rowman & Littlefield Publishers.

Warren, C. A. (2018). Empathy, teacher dispositions and preparation for culturally responsive pedagogy. *Journal of Teacher Education, 69*(2), 169–183. https://doi.org/10.1177/0022487117712487

Williams, M. T. (2020, May 23). You've committed a microaggression—now what? *Psychology Today.* https://www.psychologytoday.com/us/blog/culturally-speaking/202005/you-ve-committed-microaggression-now-what

10

Continuing the Journey and Setting Goals

Let the Lifelong Journey Begin

Well, you made it to the final chapter. How do you feel? Exhausted? Overwhelmed? Activated? Motivated? A mixture of it all? You might not even have the words to describe how you feel after reading nine chapters of heavy topics and recommendations. Critically reflecting on the questions after each chapter was likely no easy feat for you and you may have even left some for later consideration. However, as you are arriving to this chapter, it is essential to take a deep breath and recognize a single truth: the final chapter of this book doesn't mean you're now officially an antiracist. It doesn't mean that all your students are now antiracist either. No, you don't get a fancy certificate or the ability to check some imaginary box that you are done with putting in the work to be antiracist. Remember that being antiracist means that you are routinely examining everyday choices to prioritize equity (National Museum of African American History and Culture, n.d.). As antiracists, we consistently challenge the white-dominant norm. Being antiracist isn't about who you *are*, but it's more about what you *do*. What the final chapter of this book means about you and your students is that you are a teacher who has taken valuable time to dedicate to learning and changing personally and professionally. By reaching this stage, you have shown that you care deeply about your students and their roles in systemic change, for the betterment of this country.

We reach this final chapter to do two things: (1) review some major themes and consider additional resources and steps to continue the journey of being antiracist educators and (2) practice setting goals with actionable steps. Let this chapter ignite you to not take a break from these topics but strategically plan how you'll sustain the momentum you've worked hard to build over nine chapters.

Wow, We Covered So Much, But Wait, There's More!

Throughout this book, we unpacked powerful background knowledge to contextualize racial segregation in the US and systemic racism's pervasiveness, considered school culture and small steps we can take to bring antiracism to our classrooms and school communities, and specifically delved into subject areas ranging from English Language Arts (ELA) to Social-Emotional Learning. We explored some ideas that may have been brand new to you and revisited ones that may have been familiar to you. We reflected continuously, all with eyes toward our future steps. And as we know that we are not done when we close this book, let's explore some additional resources and recommendations to continue your learning.

What's Your Next Focus?

Below I have supplied suggestions for resources in a mix of formats on a variety of topics you may consider for your next steps. Some of you may feel like personal bias work is where you go from here. Some of you may feel like general teaching applications are where you'd like to head. Others may feel like they want to know more about our nation's systemic racism and the racial segregation of our schools. The lists below are a starting place for you. Believe me, I had to practice self-restraint when making an approachable list, as there are lots of recourse out there (a good problem to have). Just keep in mind that there are limited resources specific to white teachers bringing racial conversations into predominantly white elementary spaces. For obtaining more resources and for giving more suggestions, utilize this book's Facebook support group explained at the end of this chapter to explore ideas related to this specific racial dynamic. Resources below are listed in no particular order.

Resources for Working on Ourselves Personally
1. Book: *Biased: Uncovering the Hidden Prejudice That Shapes What We See, Think, and Do* by Jennifer L. Eberhardt (2020).
2. Podcast: *Code Switch* by NPR.
3. Book: *How to Be an Antiracist* by Ibram X. Kendi (2019).
4. Book: *The Racial Healing Handbook: Practical Activities to Help You Challenge Privilege, Confront Systemic Racism, and Engage in Collective Healing* by Anneliese A. Singh (2019).
5. Book: *So You Want to Talk About Race?* by Ijeoma Oluo (2020).

Resources for Working on Our Teaching
1. Book: *Unconscious Bias in Schools: A Developmental Approach to Exploring Race and Racism* by Tracey A. Benson, Sarah E. Fiarman, and Glenn E. Singleton (2020).
2. Book: *Teaching Race: How to Help Students Unmask and Challenge Racism* by Stephen A. Brookfield and Associates (2018).
3. Book: *Pedagogy of the Oppressed* by Paulo Freire (2000).
4. Book: *Why Are All the Black Kids Sitting Together in the Cafeteria? And Other Conversations About Race* by Beverly Daniel Tatum (2017).
5. Website for teaching history: facinghistory.org
6. Website for antiracist teaching practices and more: learningforjustice.org
7. For bringing current events to ELA instruction: newsela.com

Resources for Learning More About Historic and Modern Systemic Racism, CRT, and Racial Segregation of Schools
1. Podcast: *Integrated Schools Podcast* with Andrew Lefkowits and Val Brown.

2. Podcast: *School Colors Podcast* with Mark Winston Griffith and Max Freedman.
3. Book: *The Color of Law: A Forgotten History of How Our Government Segregated America* by Richard Rothstein (2018).
4. Book: *Critical Race Theory: An Introduction* by Richard Delgado and Jean Stefancic (2017).
5. Book: *Jefferson's Daughters: Three Sisters, White and Black, in a Young America* by Catherine Kerrison (2018).
6. Website and Podcast: 1619education.org from the NY Times.

And these resources are just the start. There are so many! These are just ones I have found useful personally and my list is ever-growing. And some of these resources may be useful as you delve into setting a goal for yourself and using such resources can serve as a valuable action step.

Eye of the Tiger: Set Those Goals

Let's talk goal setting. Why? Well, "teachers who set goals for themselves see significant changes in their classroom, as well as in their self-perception" (Waterford, 2020). As a teacher, I know you've heard of SMART goals, right? Specific, Measurable, Achievable, Relevant, and Time-Based goals? Before you roll your eyes at me bringing in SMART goals, hear me out. The structure of a SMART goal has some real validity in the context of antiracism work. With a concept as broad as being an antiracist educator, it's far too easy to set a lofty goal like, "I want all my students to leave my class at the end of the year knowing how to be antiracist citizens." That goal *sounds* admirable, but there's too much ambiguity there. We need to think not only about what is reasonable to expect at the end of an academic year but also what it takes to get there and what it looks like before, during, and after the action steps. Am I here to monitor that you are using the SMART goal format? No way! What I am here to do is to remind you for a goal-setting format with which you are likely familiar as an option to hold yourself accountable to ensure your goal is realistic and hopefully achievable.

I have found on my own lifelong journey of becoming an antiracist educator, asking myself some warm-up questions to get the "juices flowing" is a great start. Before we consider those questions, I'd like to address some goal-setting tips that I've found helpful. First, remember that you can start this process at any time. No reason to wait for the start of a new academic year to try and have a significant influence on your students. If you're reading this book in May and have a month left with ambitions to have an impact on your current students before they leave for the summer, then your goal needs to reflect that tight timeline and be reasonable.

Second, use your own experiences in becoming antiracist to help guide your students' journeys but respect that your journey may look different than what works for others. Just because hearing about racial injustice in the news sparked your fire, doesn't mean current events are what is going to motivate your class of seven-year-old children. Not only do we need to keep our goals age-appropriate, but we also need to consider how a variety of learners and backgrounds play significant parts in students' journeys. Maybe you want your colleagues' support in establishing a school culture that embraces antiracism, but the political climate is tense. These are all important considerations as you tailor your approach.

Third, trying to meet the goals you set may take several attempts and even the art of *setting your goal* may require trial-and-error. Hey, that's the beauty of a lifelong journey, right? We got nothing but time to figure this out, so don't let the urgency of this work lead to a sense of defeat and unwillingness to keep refining and reattempting setting goals and meeting goals. You're trying. That's what matters most. Also remember that the process is just as important as the outcomes, in every aspect of our antiracism journeys (Watt, 2020). If it's hard, you're probably doing it right. Slow, deep-rooted solutions are necessary when avoiding superficial fixes, more problems, and new issues.

Okay, now that you know to set your goal at any time (and be sure the goal reflects the timeline realistically), use your own experiences as a guideline, not a rulebook to meet your audience's needs, and to accept that trail-and-error is the name of the game, and we are ready to start! Next, we will look at five questions to help you in the goal setting and implementation process. Within this series of questions, we will explore an ingredient list for a solid antiracist teaching goal.

Question 1: Who Are You Hoping to Influence?

Let's first think about who is the focus of this goal. Are *you* the focus? If so, then maybe your goal is centered on revising your curricula and learning environment? Are your *students* the focus? If so, then possibly your goal is to have your students write about their racial biases and action steps by the end of the year. Are your *colleagues* the focus? If so, then perhaps your goal is to establish a teacher group that meets routinely to support antiracist pedagogy and resource-sharing. It's important to remember that whoever is the focus isn't the only one(s) influenced. There will be others affected as well. For example, you'll develop more as an antiracist when your students are the focus. When your colleagues are the focus, then you'll be influencing the school culture. Gotta love the ripple-effect potential of this work!

Question 2: What Would You Like Accomplished?

Now that you have your "who" decided, let's do some big dreaming. This is where we determine what we are yearning for most. Think big here, folks! I always advise to start ambitious because the remaining questions will humble you into a manageable goal. So go ahead, get those lofty dreams out of your system here. Some examples to answer this question could be: "I'd like my students to talk more openly about race" or "I want my school's culture to thoroughly embrace antiracism and recognize its white privilege." These aren't goals, yet. They are merely aspirations. However, they serve as useful grounding statements to remind yourself why you are working on the goal that you eventually set. The goal is contributing toward that aspiration.

Question 3: What Would That Aspiration Look Like if Fulfilled?

When we consider those lofty aspirations, let's break it down now into how that aspiration looks in practice. Let's use the example of students talking freely and openly about race and segment it into three signifiers that tell you the aspiration has been achieved: (1) students routinely initiate conversations about race with the teacher, peers, and whole class as they arise naturally, (2) students respect shared norms for these conversations and can uphold those expectations, and (3) students consider their whiteness and biases as part of racial conversations. This list could go on further, but these are three solid starting signifiers that the aspiration is coming true. If students are able to talk openly about race, they would be exemplifying at least these three descriptors I provided. What I want you to do now is choose one of these signifiers as the focus for crafting a goal. Save the other signifiers for future or concurrent goals to keep working toward the aspiration you identified.

Question 4: What Is a Goal That Can Make That Signifier a Reality?

Alright, now we are going to get into the nitty-gritty, and for this section, let's pretend I'm writing my goal for my fifth-graders at the start of the academic year, as that is the most common time for teacher goal setting. I aspire for my students to talk openly about race, and I chose the signifier of students respecting shared norms and upholding discussion expectations as the focus for my goal. Let's put it into some "goal language," shall we?

> Goal: *By the end of the academic year, students will respect classroom conversation norms and expectations for at least 90% of the duration of the class discussion.*

So why is this goal pretty good? It has some important qualities. It has a **clear deadline** (by the end of the academic year), it **identifies the "who"** (students) and **the desired behavior/action** (respecting and following discussion norms). It also **quantifies the results** by setting the expectation to 90% of the time when students are talking about race.

Speaking of quantifying the results, I recommend setting goals that aren't "all or nothing." Give yourself and your students some grace in this work because absolutisms in antiracism set ourselves up for failure. Remember, you're teaching young people to do something that we as adults find challenging. Expectations of perfectionism aren't realistic. When goals are unrealistic, and highly idealistic, their success rates plummet. In fact, "focusing on smaller accomplishments can bolster positive feelings, motivating us to take on more goals in the same category" (Yang et al., 2021). Smaller goals make us want to keep striving for that larger aspiration.

Remember that when you set that quantifier, you should **have in mind how you'll measure the outcomes**. How could we measure if students are following the classroom discussion norms? Don't make it overcomplicated because when those racial conversations take place, you need to be fully invested and not distracted. When I'm trying to collect data on something, I'm a lover of checklists using student rosters. You can easily make a check next to a students' name if they need a reminder of the student expectations and record how long you had to pause the discussion to remind students of expectations. Put the date on the checklist with a little note describing the discussion and takeaways so you can recall what you covered. Over the weeks, you'll get a sense if the checkmarks decreased. So, if a conversation lasts 30 minutes with the group and 3 minutes, were dedicated to a student not following expectations, pausing the discussion, and you going over the discussion norms, that means that 90% of the discussion was respectful. Is this approach highly scientific and perfect? No! But does it help you consider how the class is using their time, internalizing how to participate and uphold racial conversations, and show you which students need more reminders than others? It most certainly does!

To summarize, your goal should have the following ingredients:

1. A clear deadline, that's ambitious, but doable.
2. A focus on a set group/individual (who you strive to influence).

3. An expected behavior or action you'd like to see from the target group/individual.
4. Quantifiable results with a target number that gives you and the target group/individual some grace.
5. A sense of how you'll measure the results realistically and regularly.

Wait, did you see what happened here? We just so happened to make a SMART goal! I personally find the aforementioned series of self-reflective questions with this goal "ingredient list" more approachable to the process and more conducive for crafting future goals, too. But if the SMART formula works for you, go for it!

Question 5: What Steps Will You Take to Address This Goal?

With a solid goal in hand, this is the time to consider the smaller steps that will put it into motion. It's integral to keep your timeline in mind so that you don't overwhelm yourself with too many action steps with too little time. If I'm writing my goal at the start of the academic year, I have nine months to space out my action steps. I think that making action steps time-bound is a helpful accountability measure. I've made the mistake of writing a monster list of all the things I will do to address my goal and no sense of when to do which, how often, and then my action steps feel like a useless, jumbled mess.

Here's an example of how I could write my action steps for my example goal regarding discussion norms below. I wrote it as if I were doing this with my fifth-grade class:

1. Before the start of the school year, or in the early weeks when students are back, I'll review Chapter 4 of this book and seek out other resources on recommended classroom expectations for racial conversations. I will think about methods for making this list and how it will be used to ensure my approach matches my priorities, class age, and specific class.
2. Next, I will craft a letter to parents and caregivers before the school year, or right at the start of the year, outlining

my approach to teaching race and why I am doing so. I will show it to my school's principal before sending to elicit feedback or address any concerns they may have to ensure I have support/backup. After sending to parents, I'll address any parent concerns that may arise.
3. I will then dedicate a lesson to explicitly making the classroom rules with the class within the first couple of weeks of school. For each point that students suggest adding to the list, I will ask them to describe how they think things like "being respectful" and "listening to others" looks, sounds, and feels. I will try and ensure that students have a clear sense of how these expectations manifest into actions. This avoids our chart of expectations from being just a laundry list of things they know they should say because they hear them from adults all the time. I'll use examples to contextualize the rules for racial conversations. For example, if a student says, "don't interrupt others when you disagree" I'll say something like, "So, does that mean if I hear someone say something that makes it sound like they think one race is better than another I should let them finish before I continue?" This then leads us into how everyone will be on their own journeys, and we need to have patience with each other and attacking others who are in a different place on their journeys isn't helpful and can make us feel like we don't want to contribute if it means risking being interrupted or even yelled at.
4. Later that day, or the next day, I'll post the discussion norms in the room in a clear area that is easy to reference. I will share the list with parents and caregivers and ensure students know that this is a "living list" and we can adjust the list as needed.
5. Later that week, I'll make a pile of observation class rosters on which I can take note regarding when students do not follow the expectations. I'll put a check next to students' names to track frequency and mark the duration of the interruption (including the time it takes to reiterate the discussion norm that the student

did not follow). The form will have space for me to summarize the conversation and describe if the discussion was a planned one or one that arose spontaneously in another lesson. I'll log the percentage of time that was conducive.
6. After six weeks, I will review the logs I have and look to see if there are any trends. For example, are planned discussions less apt for interruptions than spontaneous ones? Are certain students more likely to not follow the discussion norms? Are the same discussion norms not being followed? I'll reflect on these insights and consider how I will remedy any recurring issues that may be preventing a trajectory toward 90% of racial conversations happening within the classroom expectations.
7. I'll continue this review and reflection process every six weeks and seek out additional resources and colleague support as needed. I may even ask the class, mid-way through the year, to review the discussion norms and ask them if they feel they need any updates and if they are helping us with our conversations. Could they be improved?

After reading through these action steps, I want you to notice three things. First, each action step is time-bound. My action steps have a clear flow. Second, my action steps have some statements that are open-ended for what may happen that I can't know for certain. "If…then" statements help us think through some possible scenarios before they happen, so we are better prepared. Third, the action steps lead to the end of the year, which is the endpoint of my goal. I didn't just describe what I'd do at the beginning of the year and then say I'd check on things at the end of the year either. Consistent attention to this goal holds me accountable for aiming toward progress.

I Set a Goal, Made It Happen…Now What?

Say you followed the steps outlined, crafted one heck of a goal, made manageable, time-bound action steps and you did it! The goal came to fruition. Well first, take a bow and pat yourself on the back. That's awesome! But what happens now?

Consider how you'll keep addressing the previous goal while shifting focus to a new goal. Like, I wouldn't totally disregard how often I must remind students of discussion norms the subsequent year just because I reached 90% with the class prior, right? Nope! My monitoring is hopefully routine at this point, and I can turn my gaze toward another one of the signifiers that I identified in Question 3. Our aspirations gave us great inspiration for goals, so use them as fuel for next steps and *never stop goal setting!*

Keep the Conversation Going

As a white teacher at a predominantly white school, you're far from alone. Why not take some time to connect with other educators who are grappling with the challenges you are facing? I have created a private Facebook group for readers of this book. The main intention of the group is to encourage educators who want to teach about race but need community support in the process. And let's be honest, we need a sense of community in this work.

Maybe you're a teacher in the Southern US and want to implement many of the suggestions in this book, but fear doing so due to strict policies in place. Or maybe you don't fit the description of "white teacher at a predominantly white school" but would like a space to talk about ideas related to this book. Join us! We welcome all voices who care deeply about our nation's youth fostering anti-racism for the betterment of this nation. You can find the group by searching *"Unpacking Privilege in the Elementary Classroom* Support Group." Answer a few screening questions, and you should be all set. And I'll be on there, too, to help us continue to learn and support one another through this lifelong journey.

Dr. McGowan Weighs In

The goal setting guidance in chapter 10 promotes contemplative reflection. Contemplative reflection is in alignment with the Graham Wallas Creativity Model. There are four iterative stages associated with the creativity model: (1) preparation, (2) incubation, (3) illumination, and (4) verification. In the preparation stage, you are gathering and learning from antiracist resources. The incubation stage allows you to think about the resources and how you will apply them to your antiracist education goal. The illumination phase is often referred to as the "aha" moment stage where you have a more defined idea of how to move forward. In the verification phase, you operationalize and implement a specific aspect of your antiracist goal.

Goal-Setting Prompts

Here is your space to start goal setting:

1. Who are you hoping to influence?
2. What would you like accomplished?
3. What would that aspiration look like if fulfilled?
4. What is a goal that can make that signifier a reality? Check your goal, and refine as needed by ensuring it has the following:
    a. A clear deadline, that's ambitious, but doable?
    b. A focus on a set group/individual (who you strive to influence).
    c. An expected behavior or action you'd like to see from the target group/individual.
    d. Quantifiable results with a target number that gives you and the target group/individual some grace.
    e. A sense of how you'll measure the results realistically and regularly.
    f. What steps will you take to address this goal?

    Some final reflective questions:

5. What's your next area of focus on your antiracist journey? Why does that focus make sense for you?
    1. What resources will help you with this focus?
    2. How and when will you share this book with a colleague or friend?
    3. Describe your major takeaways from this book and how you're feeling. Write it out and then share it on our Facebook group!

References

Benson, T. A., Fiarman, S. E., & Singleton, G. E. (2020). *Unconscious bias in schools: A developmental approach to exploring race and racism*. Harvard Education Press.

Brookfield, S. (2019). *Teaching race: How to help students unmask and challenge racism*. Jossey-Bass, a Wiley Brand.

Delgado, R., & Stefancic, J. (2017). *Critical race theory: An introduction* (3rd ed., Vol. 20). NYU Press.

Eberhardt, J. L. (2020). *Biased: Uncovering the hidden prejudice that shapes what we see, think, and do*. Penguin Books.

Freire, P. (2000). *Pedagogy of the oppressed* (30th anniversary ed.). Continuum.

Kendi, I. X. (2019). *How to be an antiracist*. One World, an imprint of Random House, a division of Penguin. Random House LLC.

Kerrison, C. (2018). *Jefferson's daughters: Three sisters, white and black, in a young America*. Ballantine Books.

National Museum of African American History and Culture (n.d.). *Being antiracist*. https://nmaahc.si.edu/learn/talking-about-race/topics/being-antiracist

Oluo, I. (2018). *So you want to talk about race* (First edition.). Seal Press, Hachette Book Group.

Rothstein, R. (2018). *The color of law: A forgotten hhstory of how our government segregated America*. Norton.

Singh, A. A. (2019). *The racial healing handbook: Practical activities to help you challenge privilege, confront systemic racism & engage in collective healing*. New Harbinger Publications, Inc.

Tatum, B. D. (2017). *Why are all the Bback kids sitting together in the cafeteria?: And other conversations about race: Vol. 3 trade paperback edition; Twentieth Anniversary edition*. Basic Books.

Waterford (2020, June 18). *Setting SMART teaching goals for next year*. https://www.waterford.org/education/smart-teacher-goals/

Watt, S. K. (2020, Sept. 11). Self-examination on the road to being anti-racist. *Iowa Magazine*. https://magazine.foriowa.org/story.php?ed=true&storyid=1980

Yang, H., Stamatogiannakis, A., Chattopadhyay, A., & Chakravarti, D. (2021, Jan. 4). Why we set unattainable goals. *Harvard Business Review*. https://hbr.org/2021/01/why-we-set-unattainable-goals

Index

Note: *Italic* page numbers refer to figures

academic standards 69, 99, 103, 110, 135; *see also* standards
accomplice 109
activist groups 58, 60
African American community 123, 163; *see also* community
African Americans in the Making of Early New England 77
Ali, M. 153
American Historical Association 147
anchor standards, of students 98–99; *see also* standards; students
Anderson, F. 157
Anthony, S. B. 61
anti-Black racism 156; *see also* racism
antiracism/antiracist 5, 9, 67, 69, 80, 84, 101, 108, 110–111, 126, 140, 170, 172–174, 194, 197; authentic antiracism 174; education 170; equity and 83, 86; humans 83, 172; into learning outcomes 97; lens, social-emotional learning through 184–185; SEL curriculum 185; teacher 83; into teaching 102; through writing 115–117; values/meanings 103; white identity 8; white person 47; *see also* racism
Asian cultures 53; *see also* cultures
asset mapping 177–178
atheist Soviet Union 161
authentic antiracism 174; *see also* antiracism/antiracist
Averett, N. 30

Baldwin, J. 180
Beaty, A.: *Ada Twist Scientist* 114
Bell, D. A. 36
bias(es) 2, 5, 9–14, 31, 34, 36, 46, 47, 50, 53, 54, 58, 68, 69, 71, 75, 77, 91, 92, 94, 109, 113, 115, 116, 119–122, 139, 156, 157, 169, 171, 179, 184, 186, 187, 189, 195, 199, 200
BIPOC *see* Black, Indigenous, People of Color (BIPOC)
Black History Month 45, 70, 89
Black, Indigenous, People of Color (BIPOC) 4, 9, 10, 12, 13, 15–17, 44–46, 48, 49, 51,

52, 86, 88–91, 96, 106, 111, 121, 150–152, 163, 168, 169, 171, 174, 176–178; characters and authors 112–114; communities 138; COVID-19 pandemic on 130; "gold standard" and 130; lived experiences 184; peers 188; person and relationship 188; racial empathy 182; representation 123; sense of pity for 186–187; students 127, 183, 188; systemic oppression of 185; white folks feeling bad for 184
Black Lives Matter Movement 55, 149, 173, 181; *see also* Movements
Black Muslim Organization 153
black students 2, 55, 180; *see also* students
black women 61, 128; *see also* women
Borges, A. 171, 172, 175
"Boston Busing Crisis of 1974" 22
Boston School Committee 22
boxed curriculum 157–159
Brown, O. 21
Brown v. Board of Education 20–23, 180
buy-in through facts, school culture 74–76

Calkins, L. 115
CASEL framework for SEL 185; relationship skills 187–188; responsible decision-making skills 188–189; self-awareness 186; self-management 186–187; social awareness 187
Caven, M. 185
Cayton, A. 157
centering whiteness 52, 111; *see also* whiteness
change-makers 103–106; writing as 120–122
"change-making muscle" 106
Chenoweth, E. 73
Cheryan, S. 23
Chiariello, E.: *The Whiteness Project* 85; "Why Talk About Whiteness?" 85
children 22, 52, 54, 75–77; biracial and multiracial people and 123–124; books 111; literature 112–113, 120; white children 17, 32–37, 96
civics education 14, 161–163; *see also* education
Civil Rights Era 76
Civil Rights Movement 20, 45, 55, 102, 113, 149, 152; *see also* Movements
Clark, K. 180
Clinton, H. 136
Collaborative for Academic, Social, and Emotional Learning (CASEL) Framework 15, 169
College, Career, and Civic Life (C3) Framework 163
College, Career, and Civic Life (C3) Standards 14, 163; *see also* standards

Common Core State Standards (CCSS) 12–13, 135
Common Sense Media 75
communication formats 95
community: African American 123, 163; LGBTQIA+ 131; online 15, 16; working, with school community 58–60
"condo problem" 131
conversation parameters, for students and parents 91–94
creative writing 120, 122; *see also* writing
Crenshaw, K. 36
critical race pedagogies 170; *see also* pedagogies
Critical Race Theory (CRT) 9, 34, 36–39, 45, 46, 76
Crow, J. 22
CRT *see* Critical Race Theory (CRT)
Cultural Enhancement Activities 96–97
culturally responsive pedagogies 129–135, 178; *see also* pedagogies
cultural shifting, sparking motivation for 71–73
cultures: Asian 53; and perspectives 66, 111–112; school 67–78, 82–84; United States 12, 23, 43, 105; white 129, 169, 174

decolonization and un-whitewashing social studies 149–150; curriculum 157–159; grappling with "national pride" 159–161; misrepresentation of people and events 151–154; teacher re-education 154–157; US history textbooks 150–151
"de facto" racial segregation 23
"De jure" 24
DiAngelo, R. J. 68
Dow, W. 85
Doyle, C. L. 157, 158
Doyle, J. 157, 158
Drew, C. R. 141
Dubé, L. 162

education 24, 27; civics 14, 161–163; income and lower unemployment 24, 25; racial disparities in 88; whitewashed field of 19
educators 79, 89, 91, 124, 140; science educators 138; white educators 5, 75, 85, 158; *see also* education
Educators for Anti-Racism 60
ELA *see* English Language Arts (ELA)
elementary math methods 126
emotional intelligence 189–190
emotional work: for ourselves and each other 169–171; racial work as 168–169
empathy 184; and equity 121–122; interpersonal 181; interracial 180, 182; "parochial" 180; racial *see* racial empathy; social 181–182; toward BIPOC 178–179, 181

English Language Arts (ELA) 12–14, 99, 126, 140; BIPOC characters and authors 112–114; change-makers, writing as 120–122; check "the race box" 102–103; cultures and perspectives 111–112; kid change-makers 103–106; learning about ourselves 117–120; learning opportunities and coaching for 146; race and equity 106–111; racism and antiracism 115–117; reading 103; writing 114–115
environmental justice 138; *see also* justice
environmental racism 138, 142; *see also* racism
equality 21, 24, 27, 108
equitable funding for schools 26–29; *see also* schools
equity 108; and antiracism 83, 86; empathy and 121–122; race/racism and 106–111, 116
ERI *see* ethnic-racial identity (ERI)
ethnicity 75, 108, 118
ethnic-racial identity (ERI) 186
Eurocentric views 151
"European explorers" 148
explicit lesson-based approaches 11
Exploring Lewis and Clark: Reflections on Men and Wilderness (Slaughter) 54

Exploring the Role of the School Principal in Predominantly White Middle Schools: School Leadership to Promote Multicultural Understanding (Boivin) 6

face-to-face meetings 57
faculty/staff meetings 56–57
Fair Housing Act of 1968 23
families: black family 29; CASEL framework for SEL 185; working with 58
First Amendment rights 161
Floyd, G. 181
Fourteenth Amendment to the Constitution 20
future generations, role-modeling for 46–47; personal growth *see* personal growth; professional growth *see* professional growth

gauging parental communication 95
Gay, G. 69, 129
generalization, about women 90–91; *see also* women
generational work 35–38
global majority 77, 88, 109–110, 113, 130
Goleman, D. 189
grade-level/department planning 56
grade-tailored approach 98
Graham, S. 116

Hannah-Jones, N. 156
Helms, J. E. 174
Hemmings, S. 14, 152
higher education institutions 59–60
Hispanic students 2; *see also* students

I Am Malala 12, 104, 119
Immigration Law Practitioners' Association 110
income equality 24–25, *25*
integrated residency 23–24
integrated schools 22, 32, 90; *see also* schools
interpersonal empathy 181–182; *see also* empathy
interracial empathy 180, 182
interracial social capital 30–32

Jefferson, T. 14, 152, 156
journaling 117–118
justice 108; environmental justice 138; racial equity and 100; social justice 14, 56, 58, 71, 95, 96, 108

Kendi, I. X. 186; *Stamped from the Beginning: The Definitive History of Racist Ideas in America* 156, 159
kid change-makers 103–106
A Kids Book About White Privilege (Sand) 88
King, M. L., Jr. 14, 46, 89, 152, 153

Koss, M. 113
Kucirkova, N. 183

Ladson-Billings, G. 36
Larrick, N.: "The All-White World of Children's Books" 113
learning 105; about ourselves, through writing 117–120; environment 88; outcomes, antiracism into 97
The Learning for Justice Standards 11; *see also* standards
LGBTQIA+ community 131
"Liberty and Justice for All" 161
Lies My Teacher Told Me: Everything Your American History Textbook Got Wrong (Loewen) 155
like-minded people 55–56
local businesses 58, 59, 173
local officials 58, 59
Loewen, J. 153, 157, 159; *Lies My Teacher Told Me: Everything Your American History Textbook Got Wrong* 155
Logan, E. B. 173

Mac, L. 158
Mac, T. 175
Marshall, T. 20, 21
Massachusetts Curriculum Framework 133
math and science approaches 126; culturally responsive

pedagogies 129–135; racism 135–140; STEM 126–129
McIntosh, P. 44, 87
"Me Mapping" 118
memoir writing 118; *see also* writing
microcosms of society 58
Minor, C.: "radically pro-kid" 96
Mitchell, T. 177
"model minority myth" 134
Movements: Black Lives Matter Movement 55, 149, 173, 181; Civil Rights Movement 20, 45, 55, 102, 113, 149, 152; pre-Civil Rights Movement 89; 21st Century Skills Movement 162, 180; Women's Suffrage Movement 61
multiculturalism 4, 65–67, 79–80
Munn, C. W. 31

NAACP *see* National Association for the Advancement of Colored People (NAACP)
Nabb, K. 131, 132
The Name Jar (Yangsook Choi) 53, 133
National Association for the Advancement of Colored People (NAACP) 20–21
National Endowment for the Humanities 77
"national pride," grappling with 159–161
Newhouse, K. 133
Next Generation Science Standards (NGSS) 13, 135, 137
Nolan, S. 172
nonfiction writing 120–121; *see also* writing
non-racist 48, 108; *see also* antiracism/antiracist
nonverbal cues 54
"non-whitecentric" approaches 177

"odd activist duck" 64–65
Oluo, I. 51
"one friend rule" 31, 38
online community 15, 16; *see also* community
oppression, social identity layers/systems of 50

parental buy-in, school culture 76–77
parents: and students, conversation parameters 91–94; white parent 30–33, 35, 77, 78; working with 94–97
Parks, R. 89
"parochial empathy" 180
pedagogies: critical race pedagogies 170; culturally responsive pedagogies 129–135, 178
pen-pals 182–183
people and events, misrepresentation of 151–154

"performative allyship" 51–52
personal growth 47; past, present, and future 47–50; talking and listening 50–52
perspective-taking writing 122; *see also* writing
Pew Research Center 43
"Pick a Bale of Cotton" 45
"Pint-Size Pundits Dissect Debate" 78
Plessy v. Ferguson 20
policy: equitable funding for schools 26–29; income equality 24–25, 25; integrated residency 23–24
"polygenism" 138–139
power of school culture 67–68; buy-in through facts 74–76; parental buy-in 76–77; race, in white school's culture 70–71; sparking motivation for cultural shifting 71–73; strategies 68–70; *see also* cultures
power, race, oppression and privilege (PROP) framework 71
pre-Civil Rights Movement 89; *see also* Movements
prejudice 4, 12, 30, 31, 35, 86, 89, 94, 97, 98, 105, 109, 111, 129
privilege 4, 5, 9, 11, 34, 37, 44, 45, 47, 50, 67–74, 77, 78, 87, 88, 92, 109
professional growth 52–53; working with colleagues 55–57; working with school community 58–60; working with students 53–55
"psychologically safe listening sessions" 184
public policy *see* policy

Race Cars: A Children's Book About White Privilege (Devenny) 12, 88, 110
race/racial 2, 10, 13, 15, 19, 31–33, 38, 45, 46, 52, 85, 87–91, 97, 108, 134, 139, 158, 164, 169, 175, 181, 182, 185, 188; biases 13, 199; climate 59, 105; communities 30, 132; conversations 5, 9–11, 34, 38, 55–57, 59, 65, 66, 69, 79, 95, 107, 123, 196, 200–204; disparities, in education 88; diversity 84; empathy *see* racial empathy; equity *see* racial equity; healing process 15; identities 85; injustice 105; segregation *see* racial segregation of America's schools; stereotypes; in white school's culture 70–71; *see also* stereotypes; work, as emotional work 168–169; *see also* racism
racial empathy 182; books 183–184; exposure and education 184; pen-pals 182–183; *see also* empathy
racial equity 34, 96, 120, 177, 180; committee 56; and justice 100; work 55

racial segregation of America's schools 2, 74, 109, 195; *Brown v. Board* 20–23; policy *see* policy; social complexities *see* social complexities; whitewashed field of education 19

racism 11, 45, 48, 51, 56, 76, 85, 107, 108, 110–111, 168; anti-Black racism 156; environmental racism 138; and equity 116; math and science approaches 135–140; math and science investigations 135–140; race and 126; scientific racism 138, 139; and systemic racism 88; through writing 115–117; in US 46, 86; *see also* antiracism/antiracist; racial; racism

RAND researchers 146, 148

Reid, N. 51

relationship skills 187–188

responsible decision-making skills 188–189

"revisionist history" 155

Robinson, J. 89

Roe vs. Wade 160

role-modeling, for future generations 46–47; personal growth *see* personal growth; professional growth *see* professional growth

Rufo, C. 36

Same, Same, But Different 183

Sand, B.: *A Kids Book About White Privilege* 88

Sankofa 39

school culture 67–78, 82–84; buy-in through facts 74–76; goals 83–84; parental buy-in 76–77; race, in white school's culture 70–71; sparking motivation for cultural shifting 71–73; strategies 68–70; *see also* cultures

schools 58, 161–162; Boston Public Schools 22; committee/board meetings 58–59, 71; community, working with 58–60; culture *see* school culture; equitable funding for 26–29; integrated schools 22, 32, 90; racial segregation of America's schools *see* racial segregation of America's schools; systemic racism affect 20–23; white schools 1–4, 7, 9, 19, 33, 35–38, 57–58, 65, 70–71, 84, 90, 99, 119, 182, 187–188, 205

scientific racism 138, 139; *see also* racism

Scribner, J. 68, 69

SEL approach *see* Social-Emotional Learning (SEL) approach

self-awareness 186

self-care for white antiracists 171–175; *see also* antiracism/antiracist

self-management 186–187

self-reflection 68, 119

service-learning 177–178
Sims-Bishop, R. 112
Slaughter, T. P.: *Exploring Lewis and Clark: Reflections on Men and Wilderness* 54
SMART goal 197, 202
Smith, D. 92
social awareness 187–189
social capital 29–33
social change 28, 105, 115, 119
social class 61, 74
social complexities: battling white supremacy 33–35; social capital, importance of 29–33; white classrooms with white teachers 35–38
social-emotional development 189–190
Social-Emotional Learning (SEL) approach 15, 169; avoiding burnout and maintaining motivation 175–178; CASEL framework for *see* CASEL framework for SEL; emotional support, for ourselves and each other 169–171; empathy 178–182; racial empathy 182–184; racial work 168–169; self-care for white antiracists 171–175; through antiracist lens 184–185
social-emotional tactics and insights 82
social-emotional well-being 189
social empathy 181–182; *see also* empathy

social identity 50, 61, 80
social justice 14, 56, 58, 71, 95, 96, 108; *see also* justice
Social Justice Standards 97, 99; *see also* standards
social studies/civics approaches 146–149; civics education 161–163; decolonization and un-whitewashing *see* decolonization and un-whitewashing social studies
Socratic seminars 78, 136
Song, E. 141
sparking motivation for cultural shifting 71–73
Stamped from the Beginning: The Definitive History of Racist Ideas in America (Kendi) 156
standards: academic standards 69, 99, 103, 110, 135; anchor standards, of students 98–99; College, Career, and Civic Life Standards 14, 163; Common Core State Standards 12–13, 135; The Learning for Justice Standards 11; Next Generation Science Standards 13, 135, 137; Social Justice Standards 97, 99
Stanton, E. C. 61
Stearns, P. N. 31
STEM 126–129
stereotypes 10, 31, 34, 52, 109, 129, 134, 136, 179; racial 139; verbalizing 53

stress management 187
student-generated parameters 169
students 12, 86, 88, 105, 121, 159, 177, 178, 199, 200; academic knowledge and skill sets 179; anchor standards of 98–99; BIPOC 127; black students 2, 55, 180; and parents, conversation parameters 91–94; reading 103; US Public School students 2, 3; white students 2, 3, 6, 76, 130, 185, 186; working with 53–55
summer professional development program 77
"sustainable strategies for activism" 175
systemic racism 19, 55, 129–135, 168, 175, 195; affect schools 20–23; racism and 88; *see also* antiracism/antiracist; racism

Tatum, B. D. 7
teachers 46, 74, 87, 89, 97, 128, 159; and antiracist humans 172; gateway opportunities for 11; preparation program 59; re-education 154–157; in Southern US 205; in urban settings 4; white teachers 2, 5–7, 9–10, 15–16, 21, 35–38, 43, 85, 106, 205
"Teachers Pay Teachers" 148

"10 R's of Talking About Race" 92
"3.5% Rule" 73–74
"trial-and-error" system 5, 198–199
Trump, D. 36, 136
21st Century Skills Movement 162, 180; *see also* Movements

universal racial equity 134
US/America: character 85; culture 12, 23, 43, 105; *see also* cultures; education system 26; history textbooks 150–153, 163; Public School students 2, 3; racism in 46, 86; systems and institutions 85; whiteness society 85, 86

verbalizing stereotypes 53; *see also* stereotypes
vicious cycle 23, 27–29
Vietnam War 153–154

white: antiracists, self-care for 171–175; *see also* antiracism/antiracist; children 17, 32, 33, 35–37, 96; *see also* children; classrooms 35–38; culture 129, 169, 174; *see also* cultures; educators 5, 75, 85, 158; *see also* educators; identity 8, 34, 174–175; parents 22, 30–33, 35, 37, 45, 71, 74, 77; people 29, 50–52, 111, 178–179; privilege 36, 37, 44, 47, 67, 74, 87, 88, 109,

118, 147, 175, 187, 199; racial identity 174; saviorism 51, 138, 177; schools 1–4, 7, 9, 19, 33, 35–38, 57, 58, 65, 70–71, 84, 90, 99, 119, 182, 187, 188, 205; *see also* schools; spaces 37, 46, 48, 50, 51; students 2, 3, 6, 76, 130, 185, 186; *see also* students; supremacy 33–35, 82, 110, 171, 174, 185; teachers 2, 5–7, 9, 10, 15–16, 21, 35–38, 43, 85, 106, 205; *see also* teachers; woman 5, 44, 50, 51, 113, 127, 168

white-dominant norm 194

whiteness 8, 26, 45, 46, 50, 52, 84–88, 111, 174; in American society 85; centering whiteness 52, 111; culturally responsive pedagogies 129–135; white identity 86

whitewashed field of education 19

women: black women 61, 128; generalization about 90–91; white woman 5, 44, 50, 51, 113, 127, 168

Women's Suffrage Movement 61; *see also* Movements

"wonder journals" 117

workforce racial isolation 31

working: with colleagues 55–57; on day-to-day student 83; with families 58; with parents 94–97; with school community 58–60; in STEM 128; with students 53–55

World Wildlife Fund 104

writing 114–115; as change-makers 120–122; creative writing 120, 122; learning about ourselves through 117–120; memoir writing 118; nonfiction writing 120–121; racism and antiracism through 115–117

Wyche, V. 141

Yangsook Choi: *The Name Jar* 133

Zinn Education Project 55, 60

Zou, L. X. 23

For Product Safety Concerns and Information please contact our EU
representative GPSR@taylorandfrancis.com
Taylor & Francis Verlag GmbH, Kaufingerstraße 24, 80331 München, Germany

www.ingramcontent.com/pod-product-compliance
Lightning Source LLC
Chambersburg PA
CBHW070253230426
43664CB00014B/2515